"*Disciplines of Modernity* is a unique, thought-provoking, and challenging book. It makes an important intervention in the fields of social sciences and humanities by speaking across disciplines and archives. The work takes us forward from the moment of postcolonial and decolonial critique and recasts the framework within which scholars of/ from the global south and the global north may henceforth converse."

Prathama Banerjee, *Professor, Centre for the Study of Developing Societies, Delhi*

"This is an innovative and inviting, powerful and provocative book. Abjuring the usual 'guarantees' of academic analysis, Dube conjoins intimacy and affect with structure and process. In the work, predilections of the postcolonial are interwoven with the contradictions of modernity, the contentions of disciplines are bound to ambiguities of the archive, and accumulation and development are crisscrossed by loss and excess."

Mario Rufer, *Professor, Universidad Autónoma Metropolitana, México*

I0123569

Disciplines of Modernity

Scrupulously based in anthropology and history – and drawing on social theory and critical thought – this book revisits the disciplines, archives, and subjects of modernity.

There are at least three interleaving emphases here. To begin with, the work rethinks institutionalized formations of anthropology and history – together with "archives" at large – as themselves intimating disciplines of modernity. Understood in the widest senses of the terms, these disciplines are constitutively contradictory.

Moreover, the study interrupts familiar projections of modern subjects as molded *a priori* by a disenchanted calculus of interest and reason. It tracks instead the affective, embodied, and immanent attributes of our varied worlds as formative of subjects of modernity, sown into their substance and spirit.

Finally, running through the book is a querying of entitlement and privilege that underlie social terrains and their scholarly apprehensions – articulating at once distinct elites, pervasive plutocracies, and modern "scholasticisms."

Saurabh Dube is Professor-Researcher, Distinguished Category, El Colegio de México, Mexico City.

Routledge Focus on Modern Subjects

Series Editor: **Saurabh Dube,** *Professor-Researcher, Distinguished Category, El Colegio de México*

The volumes in this Focus series shall explore quotidian claims made on the modern – understood as idea and image, practice and procedure – as part of everyday articulations of modernity in South Asia, Africa, and the Middle East. Here, the category-entity of the subject refers not only to social actors who have been active participants in historical processes of modernity, but as equally implying branch of learning and area of study, topic and theme, question and matter, and issue and business. Our effort is to explore such modern subjects in a range of distinct yet overlaying ways.

The titles in the series address earlier understandings of the modern and recent reconsiderations of modernity by focusing on a clutch of common and critical questions. Indeed, our bid is to carefully query aggrandizing representations of modernity "as" the West, while prudently tracking the place of such projections in the commonplace unravelling of the modern in Global Souths today.

Other books in this series

Fluid Modernity
The Politics of Water in the Middle East
Gilberto Conde

The Dazzle of the Digital
Unbundling India Online
Meghna Bal and Vivan Sharan

For more information about this series, please visit: www.routledge.com/ Routledge-Focus-on-Modern-Subjects/book-series/RFOMS

Disciplines of Modernity
Archives, Histories, Anthropologies

Saurabh Dube

R Routledge
Taylor & Francis Group

LONDON AND NEW YORK

First published 2023
by Routledge
2 Park Square, Milton Park, Abingdon, Oxon OX14 4RN

and by Routledge
605 Third Avenue, New York, NY 10158

Routledge is an imprint of the Taylor & Francis Group, an information business

© 2023 Saurabh Dube

British Library Cataloguing-in-Publication Data
A catalogue record for this book is available from the British Library

ISBN: 978-1-032-38939-4 (hbk)
ISBN: 978-1-032-38940-0 (pbk)
ISBN: 978-1-003-34756-9 (ebk)

DOI: 10.4324/9781003347569

Typeset in Times New Roman
by codeMantra

Contents

Series Editor's Statement   ix
Preface   xiii

1   Introduction   1

2   Rethinking Disciplines: Anthropology and History   19

3   Figures of Dissonance: Dalit Religions and
    Anthropological Archives   45

4   Subjects of Privilege: Entitlements and Affects
    in Plutocratic Worlds   65

5   Issues of Immanence: Modern Scholasticism
    and Academic Entitlement   86

    References   103
    Index   131

Series Editor's Statement

Routledge Focus on Modern Subjects has a broad yet particular purpose. It seeks to explore quotidian claims made on the *modern* – understood as idea and image, practice and procedure – as part of everyday articulations of modernity in South Asia, the Middle East, and Africa. Here, the category-entity of the *subject* also has wide purchase. It refers not only to social actors who have been active participants in historical processes of modernity, but equally implies branch of learning and area of study, topic and theme, question and matter, and issue and business. The series attempts to address such modern subjects in a range of distinct yet overlaying ways.

Questions of modernity have always been bound to issues of being/becoming modern. These themes have been discussed in various ways for long now.[1] For convenience, we might distinguish between two broad, opposed tendencies. On the one hand, over the past few centuries, it is the West/Europe that has been seen as the locus and the habitus of the modern and modernity. Such a West is imaginary yet tangible, principally envisioned in the image of the North Atlantic world. And it is from these arenas that modernity and the modern appear as spreading outwards to transform other, distant and marginal, peoples in the mold and the wake of the West. On the other hand, such propositions have been contested by rival claims, including especially from within Romanticist and anti-modernist dispositions. Here, if the modern and modernity have been often understood as intimating the fundamental fall of humanity, everywhere, so too have the aggrandizements of an analytical reason been countered through procedures of a hermeneutic provenance.

Needless to say, these contending tendencies have for long each found imaginative articulations, and I provide indicative examples from our own times. The work of philosophers such as Jürgen Habermas and Charles Taylor and historians such as Reinhart Koselleck and Hans

Ulrich Gumbrecht have opened up the exact terms, textures, and transformations of modernity and the modern. At the same time, they have
arguably located the constitutive conditions of these phenomena in
Western Europe and Euro-America. In contrast, anti-modernist sensibilities have found innovative elaborations in, say, the "critical tradition-
alism" of Ashis Nandy in South Asia; and the querying of Eurocentric
thought has been intriguingly expressed by the scholars of the "coloniality of knowledge" and "decoloniality of power" in Latin America.
These powerful positions variously rest on assumptions of innocence
before and outside Europe and the West, modernity and the modern.

Engaging with yet going beyond such prior emphases, recent work
on modernity has charted new directions, departures that have served
to foreground questions of modernity in academic agendas and on
intellectual horizons, more broadly. I indicate four critical trends.
First and foremost, there have been works focusing on different
expressions of the modern and distinct articulations of modernity as
historically grounded and/or culturally expressed, articulations that
query *a priori* projections and sociological formalisms underpin-
ning the category-entity. Second, there are distinct studies that have
diversely explored issues of "early" and "colonial" and "multiple"
and "alternative" modernity/modernities. Third, we find imaginative
ethnographic, historical, and theoretical explorations of modernity's
conceptual cognates such as globalization, capitalism, and cosmopolitanism as well as of attendant issues of state, nation, and democracy.
Fourth and finally, there have been varied explorations of the enchantments of modernity and of the magic of the modern, understood not
as analytical errors but as formative of social worlds. These studies
have ranged from the elaborations of the fetish of the state, the sacred
character of modern sovereignty, the uncanny of capitalism, and the
routine enticements of modernity through to the secular magic of
representational practices such as entertainment shows, cinema, and
advertising.

Routledge Focus on Modern Subjects engages and exceeds, takes forward and departs from such concerns in its own manner. To start off, its
titles address the queries and concepts entailed in earlier explorations
of the modern and recent reconsiderations of modernity by focusing
on a clutch of common and critical questions. These issues turn on the
everyday elaborations of the modern, the quotidian configurations of
modernity, in South Asia, Africa, and the Middle East. Next, rather
than simply asserting the empirical plurality of modernity and the
modern, the series approaches the routine, even banal, expressions of

the modern as registering contingency, contradiction, and contention as lying at the core of modernity. Further, it only follows that our bid is not to indolently exorcize aggrandizing representations of modernity *as* the West, but to prudently track instead the play of such projections in the commonplace unraveling of the modern in global souths today. Finally, such procedures not only recast broad questions – for instance of cosmopolitanism and globalization, state and citizenship, Eurocentrism and Nativism, aesthetics and authority – by approaching them through routine renderings of the modern in contemporary worlds. They also stay with the dense, exact expressions of modernity yet all the while attending to their larger, critical implications, prudently thinking *both* down to the ground.

In keeping with the spirit of the series, all its titles stand informed by specific renderings – as well as focused rethinking – of key categories and processes. Two exact instances. In different ways, concepts and processes of power and politics alongside those of community and identity variously run through the *Focus Series on Modern Subjects.* Here, neither power nor politics are rendered as signifying solely institutional relations of authority centering on the state and its subjects. Rather, the bid is to articulate these as equally embodying diffuse domains and intimate arrangements of authority and desire, including their seductions and subversions. Actually, as parts of such force-fields, state and government, their policy and program might now assume twinned dimensions in understandings of modern subjects. Here can be found densely embodied disciplinary techniques toward forming and transforming subjects-citizens, where such protocols and their reworking by citizens-subjects no less register the shaping of authority by anxiety, uncertainty, and alterity, of the structuring of command by deferral, difference, and displacement.

At the same time, the series approaches community and identity as modern processes of meaning and authority, located at the core of nation and globalization. This is to say that instead of approaching identity and community as already given entities that are principally antithetical to modernity, this cluster explores communities and identities as wide-ranging processes of formations of subjects, expressing collective groupings and particular personhoods. Defined within social relationships of production and reproduction, appropriation and approbation, and power and difference, emergent identities, cultural communities, and their mutations appear now as essential elements in the quotidian constitution, expressions, and transformations of modern subjects.

Note

1 The discussion in this Foreword of different understandings of modernity (and the modern) draws upon a wide range of scholarship. Instead of cluttering the short piece with numerous references, indicated here are a few of the works of the series editor that have addressed these themes – in dialogue with relevant literatures – and that back the claims made ahead. Needless to say, prior arguments and emphases are being cryptically condensed and radically rearranged for the present purposes. Saurabh Dube, *Subjects of Modernity: Time-Space, Disciplines, Margins* (Manchester: Manchester University Press, 2017); Saurabh Dube, *Stitches on Time: Colonial Textures and Postcolonial Tangles* (Durham and London: Duke University Press, 2004); and Saurabh Dube, *After Conversion: Cultural Histories of Modern India* (New Delhi: Yoda Press, 2010). Consider also, Saurabh Dube (ed.), *Enchantments of Modernity: Empire, Nation, Globalization* (London: Routledge, 2009); and Saurabh Dube (ed.), *Handbook of Modernity in South Asia: Modern Makeovers* (New Delhi: Oxford University Press, 2011).

Preface

As the Introduction ahead discusses, the remote intimations of this book lay in strange circumstances, contrary verities, intimate tragedies. At the same time, it is through the pathos of the pandemic that its connected chapters acquired shape and assumed substance. Here, apparently discrete subjects appear articulated and interpellated by mutual emphases, overlapping arguments. All of this defines the principal purpose of *Disciplines of Modernity*.

Let me confess to an initial unease at having my own book appear in a series of which I am the editor. The doubts were dispelled as I understood how this work takes forward the aims and concerns of the common cluster in critical conversation with its other titles – already published, forthcoming soon, under contract, and presently under consideration. I offer sincere thanks to Aafreen Ayub, my splendid editor and worthy co-conspirator at "Routledge Focus on Modern Subjects." She not only encouraged me to consider the fit between *Disciplines of Modernity* and the series, but also assiduously masterminded the means by which the anonymity of the review process of the manuscript remained entirely uncompromised. Aafreen herself called the sole shots in deciding the referees. I owe her many more breakfasts, hopefully followed by other walks in the Lodhi Gardens.

Upon receiving the reports, it was the wider comments and precise suggestions of the anonymous readers that fractally unraveled their identities to me. I am deeply indebted to the generous reading and thoughtful suggestions of these remarkable intellects that have made the book a better one. For discussion and dialogue, I would like to thank also Prathama Banerjee, Michael Herzfeld, Mario Rufer, Zine Magubane, and Ishita Banerjee Dube. Others who contributed to this book have been acknowledged in its individual chapters. As for Natalia Wood, no number of words can express my immense gratitude to her. In equal parts friend and savior, research-assistant and critical-discussant, Natalia's presence in this book is a formidable one. I look forward to being of assistance toward Natalia's own imaginative work in the years ahead.

Rather earlier versions of some of the chapters in front have appeared in distinct publications of the Oxford University Press (out of both, New York and New Delhi), Routledge (London), and in the *Economic and Political Weekly*: I gratefully acknowledge their use here in other avatars, different incarnations.

1 Introduction

There are times in life when it is impossible to find anew affect and understanding without losing prior beliefs and certainties. Several of the modern subjects that inhabit and impel this book – articulating and enabling its arguments, expressing and interrogating its emphases – intimated themselves to me around a decade ago. At that time, as dementia extolled its cost, light was slowly fading from my mother's eyes. Alongside, in the wake of the global economic crisis that began in 2008, the "1 per cent" (actually, the plutocratic 0.1 per cent) announced themselves, across latitudes and longitudes, as the doers and un-doers of relentless capital, the world, the globe, the planet. Possibly it was this conjunction of the impending death of the remaining parent alongside the growing salience of an entitled elite that led me to a curious research project. Namely, a study of my own high-school cohort, principally subjects of privilege, a return journey of sorts to childhood and adolescence, innocence and its absence, the past and the present.

That project has expanded in the last few years to cover many more modern subjects – also of affect and entitlement, friendship and prejudice, memory and hierarchy, gender and sexuality – that inhabit places of prerogative (Chapter 4). Unsurprisingly, at stake equally are the terms of privilege that course through my own routine life-worlds, of intellectual entitlement and cultural capital, long glimpsed but now charged with a discrete force, a distinct gravity. Here are arenas where university presidents and academic regents, ambassadors and diplomats, increasingly come to imagine themselves in the likeness of the plutocratic untouchable set, albeit with (relentless) wealth and its command substituted by (institutional) authority and its arrogance.

Throughout, conjoining fieldwork and homework, my instinctive, routine ethnographies of the academic and intellectual everyday have betokened other verities. To wit, the very smell and sniffing of privilege and hierarchy insinuate anxieties of entitlement and authority, which

DOI: 10.4324/9781003347569-1

often rise with heightened mediocrity and connected conceits. Such are the disagreeable quotidian worlds in which this work was written. But we should not forget that the provocations of these domains have led me in curios keys to other, overlapping modern subjects: of routine scholasticism, aggrandizing transcendence, and worldly immanence (Chapter 5); of Dalit dissonance and anthropological archives (Chapter 3); and of history and anthropology not merely as modern disciplines but as disciplines of modernity, bearing the archival traces and tracks of the latter (Chapter 2). All this should soon become clear. As I bring this book to a close, the point is that longing and loss have undone older truths and instated unsettling actualities.

Overture

Across the last three decades, my research, writing, and teaching have variously combined history, anthropology, and social theory. In such endeavor, I have focused chiefly on subjects of a South Asian provenance yet drawn these into dialogue with other geo-political arenas, including of course Latin American ones. Alongside, joining important exercises in different fields, I have approached the issues at stake in terms of wider considerations of critical thought and searching method. Undertaking such steps, I have been struck, again and again, by the remarkable persistence of overlapping exceptionalisms in academes at large. Indeed, despite the many remarkable departures in the critical human-sciences for long now, these exceptionalisms are simultaneously manifest in the lasting epistemic privilege accorded to Euro-American frames *and* as enduring *a priori* alterities sown into Asian, African, Latin American, and other subordinate terrains.

  Disciplines of Modernity critically unravels such concerns by turning to three connected congeries of considerations. First, the work seeks to understand anthropologies and histories as themselves insinuating *disciplines of modernity*, understanding the terms in capacious yet critical ways that extend these institutionalized enquiries beyond conventional claims of their being merely *modern disciplines*. Second, it attends simultaneously to subjects of privilege and precarity, particularly as turning upon elites and Dalits. Finally, the book explores figures of affect and entitlement, including as drawing in the terms and textures of (earthly) immanence and (modern) scholasticism. Each of these distinct yet overlapping procedures engages, expresses, and articulates often cunning, even uncanny, *archives of modernity*, which straddle tacit meanings, explicit authority, and their pervasive admixtures.

At stake throughout are bids that stay with in order to think through abiding exceptionalisms, aggrandizing analytics, and knee-jerk refusals of many-sided modern scholasticisms, which characterize academic and everyday arenas. Here, I have in mind the various uniformities of Eurocentric accounts; the split exceptionalisms of area-studies-as-usual; the self-congratulatory attributes of nativism(s) that abound; and the unbalanced dystopias/utopias of significant strains of radical criticism and anti-essentialist energies. Registering that there are of course key differences within and across these wide-ranging perspectives, my point concerns what the positions might yet share, including the wider oversight of their own claims upon intellectual transcendence.[1]

Allow me to sharpen my earlier emphases concerning these questions.[2] On the one hand, without belaboring the obvious, lingering "meta-geographical" assumption frequently casts the many reaches of the non-West as innately different and all too distant. These grounds bear an inherent exoticism or embody an inevitable lack or, of course, articulate both at once. Straddling the logics of essential sameness in history or/and innate difference in culture, the terrains at issue are principally envisioned in the mirrors of an exclusive modernity. Unsteadily reflected in the likenesses of universal history, to be found here are hierarchical conjunctions of time and space (Dube 2017a).

On the other hand, the challenges to such presumptions, whether rendered as anti-essentialist thinking or rehearsed in significant strands of radical critique, can no less elaborate their own species of exceptionalisms. Here, the force of criticism serves to turn power and dominance – of empire and nation, colony and modernity, the state and the West, globalization and the North – into a dystopian totality, a distant enemy. Against these dissonant dystopias are unsteadily pitted the ethics of alterity and the subaltern, the innocence of difference and resistance, each articulated as un-recuperated particulars, all *a priori* antidotes to authority (Dube 2016, 2017a, 2019a).[3]

Rather than simply dismissing such tendencies as analytical nightmares, easily exorcised through astute imaginaries, it is salient to carefully consider their formidable presumption.[4] These tasks are not only empirical but already critical. Here, to face up to exceptionalisms entails questioning projections of power as insinuating routine sameness and/or inherently dystopian totalities, while equally querying assumptions of alterity as intimating innate exoticisms or/and forceful antidotes to authority. It also means tracking the interplay between power and meaning, dominance and dissonance, and discipline and recalcitrance. Such prudent probing untangles formations of power as shot through with difference, revealing the presence of intimacies, ambivalences, and anxieties of authority. It equally unravels procedures of alterity as inflected by authority, registering the place of difference, subaltern, and resistance as subjects of power. These modes of understanding form part of what I have called a "history without warranty" (Dube 2004a), considerations that acquire also a different valence in this book, including at its end.

Now, to apprehend and eschew exceptionalisms of distinct stripes invites resolute struggles with scholastic protocols of modern knowledge. Minimally apprehended, these widespread modern scholasticisms pervasively substitute the author's own "ought" for the contentious "is" that inhabits the world, as Chapter 5 discusses. There I elaborate also my particular use of the term scholasticism under modernity, despite the evolution of modern Western thought in self-conscious opposition to prior scholasticisms of the twelfth to sixteenth centuries. Now, if scholasticisms could variously exceed the pejorative apprehensions that Renaissance humanists had of them (Pieper 2001), scholastic knowledges could also be implicated in wide-ranging processes of mercantile capitalism (Bentancor 2017). The point is that interleaving important emphases of Pierre Bourdieu (1984, 2000) and key concerns of Jacques Rancière (1989, 1991, 2004) my use of modern scholasticism refers to persistent protocols of knowledge and knowing that articulate their particular case as the general story, all the while exorcising their own conditions of possibility.

How might we face up to modern scholasticisms? Or, put in terms of a prescient interlocutor, what would be a "radical critique" adequate to intellectual and academic elitism? My own bid is to understand entitlement and privilege in order to unlearn privilege and entitlement. I do this in a spirit that refuses to see the object-subject of its critique as a distant enemy, which is to say as the dystopian habitus of intellectual adversaries. Rather, my concern is with the tangible and visceral intimacies of scholasticism that are routinely inhabited in academe, eliding our entitlement by repeatedly turning to the overwhelmingly analytical, the chiefly cerebral, the endlessly self-congratulatory. Moreover, at stake is the challenge of engaging with, entering into, distinct protocols of social theory, based not on their meta-geographical origins but on their critical-imaginative possibilities. Here, under issue is the importance of admitting the necessary not-one-ness of global souths and social worlds at large – including, the inadequacy yet indispensability of European thought – not merely in empirical manners but in critical ways. Finally, all of this is far from privileging epistemology as the principal mode of political-academic-whatever engagement, reducing actual struggles to battles over conceptual purity, themselves overwrought protocols of scholastic reason. Rather, I am indicating actions and ideas, teaching and writing, ethic and affect, conduct and value – inside the academy, outside it, and at their intersections – as being vitally committed to compelling non-hierarchy, unhesitant democratic-horizons, formative anti-vanguardism, and endless undoing of abounding *a priories*. That is, as open to and capable of rethinking closely held premises, principles, and practices, based on concrete issues and particular struggles. All of this is not my "ought" but my "is," the costs be damned.[5]

There is even more to the picture. For, in apprehending and exploring academic and everyday arenas, it becomes critical to stay longer with corporeal, affective, sensuous ways of experiencing/knowing/being (Ahmed 2004; Clough and Halley 2007; Stewart 2007; see also Mitchell 2005; and Mahmood 2011). These put a question mark on pervasive presumptions of fully fabricated subjects, ever possessed of an already-intimated reason. Yet such querying does not portray subjects as being pre-social in any sense, located as they are in necessarily heterogeneous yet overlapping life-worlds.

Asked differently, can apprehensions of social life eschew starting off with the "bounded, intentional subject" even as it foregrounds "embodiment and sensuous life" (Mazzarella 2009: 291)? Here, might "affective circumstances" take *experiential* precedence over, while being constitutively coeval with, more formal procedures of reason? Indeed, with "subject and sense" shaped by elements of experience (Rajchman 2001: 15), might we also take a cue from Gadamer – who articulates of course a distinct intellectual tradition – in order to ask: How do we open ourselves to the awareness of "being exposed to the labors of history" that "precede the objectifications of documentary historiography" (H-G Gadamer, cited in Bauman 1992: ix–x) and explanatory anthropology?[6]

It should be clear that I am not speaking of the affective and the extra-analytical – each ever embodied, at once in spirit and substance – as a sort of "return of the repressed" under modernity (Mazzarella 2009: 293). Rather, I am referring to the affective, the extra-analytical, and the embodied as *routinely woven* into our everyday and academic modern worlds.[7] These each ever announce, well, immanence.

I mean by immanence a recognition of value properties that actually inhabit the world and not just as detached projections of words and images (Chapter 5). Here, categories (academic and everyday), far from being seen as principally instrumental explanatory devices, are approached instead as constitutive attributes of social worlds, which also can variously bear value properties. These value properties of objects and subjects, categories and imaginaries make claims upon us, inviting and inciting meaningful practices. How might such immanent attributes of social life – including the place and play of longing and loss, color and smell, the sensitive and the sensuous – be drawn into descriptions, woven into narratives, rather than pursue a "sense-less science" (Fabian 2000: ix)?[8]

Unraveling Emphases

Animated by such spirit and sensibility, *Disciplines of Modernity* makes discrete incisions and specific sutures upon the corpus of "modern subjects," as articulated by the aspirations of the present series. Through close, connected, and critical readings it formatively juxtaposes historical and anthropological knowledges, Dalit and elite protagonists, immanent and scholastic reason(s), academic and everyday arenas, and analytical and affective subjects. At stake are re-visitations of the disciplines, archives, and habitations of modernity that ask questions of routine manners of seeing and doing in our worlds today.

Before proceeding further, it might not be out of place for a thumb-nail sketch of how I approach and apprehend modernity. Now, upon my reading, modernity is not the sole product of, say, Cartesian dualities or a singular Enlightenment predicated upon aggrandizing analytics or the imperial endeavors of the British, the French, and the Dutch after the eighteenth century or, indeed, all of the above. Rather, the modernity of the Enlightenment (with its acute interplay between race and reason) came only after the modernity of the Renaissance (with its interleaving of metaphysical instrumentalism and mercantile capitalism), quite as the constitutive violence of modernity of later colonialisms was preceded by modern genocides of the empires of Americas at large. The point is that the processes of modernity since the sixteenth century need to be approached as being constitutively contradictory, contingent, and contested: protocols that are incessantly articulated yet also critically out of joint with themselves.[9] And it is precisely these procedures that emerge expressed by subjects of modernity, some of whom are modern subjects of course.[10]

This book begins by rethinking institutionalized formations of anthropology and history – together with modern archives – as themselves intimating disciplines of modernity. To offer this claim is to untangle both these enquiries as severally shaped by the *Ur*-opposition between the "primitive/native" and the "civilized/modern." Here are to be found genealogically the looming impress of empire and nation, race and reason, and their incessant interplay. At the same time, at stake are analytical and hermeneutical orientations, romanticist and progressivist dispositions, and their formidable entanglements. Understood in their widest senses of the term, these disciplines are constitutively contradictory. This is true also of archives, including/ especially in considerations – as in this book – of anthropological and historical knowledges, varieties of social theory, and the repositories of research we ourselves make and uncertainly inhabit as all intimating archival formations. I shall soon return to these issues of disciplines and archives.

The point now concerns two interleaving emphases. On the one hand, *Disciplines of Modernity* interrupts familiar projections of modern subjects as molded *a priori* by a disenchanted calculus of interest and reason. It acknowledges instead the affective and embodied, sensuous and immanent attributes of modern worlds, routinely sown into the substance and spirit of their subjects and habitations. On the other hand, running through the book is a querying of entitlement and privilege that form the core of our social worlds and their scholarly apprehensions – at once drawing in distinct elites, discrete plutocracies, academic cultures, and modern scholasticisms.

Disciplines and Archives

Pervasive presumptions in the human sciences project anthropology and history as taken-for-granted divisions of knowledge, whose relationship is then tracked as being vexed but constructive. This can lead also to the demarcation of specialized fields such as "historical anthropology" and "ethnographic history," disciplinary enquiries into "history of anthropology" and "historiography of history," and broad considerations of the "anthropology of history" and "ethnography of anthropology." At the same time, what does it mean to rethink history and anthropology as *disciplines of modernity*, bearing the archival tracks of its protocols and procedures?

Beginning with the Enlightenment and Romanticism, historical and anthropological knowledges each appeared as mutually if variously shaped by overarching distinctions between the "primitive/native" and the "civilized/modern." It followed that the wide-ranging dynamic of empire and nation, race and reason, and analytical and hermeneutical orientations underlay the fraught emergence of anthropology and history as institutionalized enquiries in the second half of the nineteenth century. And so too, across much of the twentieth century and through its wider upheavals, it was by attempting uneasily to break with these genealogies yet never fully even escaping their impress that these enquiries staked their claims as modern disciplines. This entailed especially their discrete expressions of time and space, culture and change, tradition and modernity. Unsurprisingly, the mutual makeovers of history and anthropology since the 1970s have thought through the formidable conceits of both these knowledges while reconsidering questions of theory and method, object and subject, and the archive and the field. The newer emphases have imaginatively articulated issues of historical consciousness and marginal communities, colony and nation, empire and modernity, race and slavery, alterity and identity, indigeneity and heritage, and the state and the secular. Yet, such valuable departures have often also been accompanied by an uncertain reproduction of the oppositions between power and difference, authority and alterity, even as the haunting antinomies between the "savage/native" and the "civilized/modern" have found mutating expressions within emergent hierarchies of otherness.

All of this underlies anthropology and history as constitutively contradictory, necessarily split, and formatively contended disciplines of modernity. As archive and practice, these disciplinary formations have at once inscribed and unraveled modernity's traces and tracks. At stake are the distinct meanings – and their key conjunctions – of the term discipline, which I derive freely from the Merriam-Webster Online Dictionary. As noun: "a field of study"; "a rule or system of rules governing conduct or activity"; [obsolete] "instruction"; "control gained enforcing obedience or order"; "orderly prescribed conduct or pattern of behavior"; "self-control"; "training that corrects, molds, or perfects the mental faculties or moral character." As transitive verb: "to train or develop by instruction and exercise, including in self-control"; "to bring [a collective] under control"; "to impose order upon."

We just noted that the institutional emergence of anthropology and history as modern enquiries occurred in the second half of the nineteenth century. But their provenance lay in prior formations of power and knowledge as well as their contentions and criticisms, turning upon Enlightenment and counter-Enlightenment, reason and romanticism, and empire and nation. Talal Asad (1993: 269) has reminded us that at stake in these terrains were motivated (albeit diverse) protocols "not simply of looking and recording but of recording and remaking" the world, as well as of the challenges to such propositions and practices. This is the site and scene upon which the different registers of the notion of discipline came to be at once entwined and unraveled in decidedly contradictory and contended manners.

On the one hand, it was the demarcations of the "Age of Reason" that made possible Western academic enquiries "to break almost wholly from their African, Asian and Middle Eastern predecessors to proclaim themselves self-birthed.... Here, race equals place, and all other races, like all other places, are inferior to (white) Europeans and Europe" (Wright nd: 4). On the other hand, these were also the grounds on which the aggrandizements and conceits of reason came to be queried and exceeded not only by counter-Enlightenment and romanticist thinkers but equally by contending strains of the Enlightenment, especially as expressed by philosophers such as Hume and Kant (Kelley 1998; Pococok 1999; Berlin 2001; Porter 2001; Zammito 2002. See also, Becker 1932; McMahon 2002; Muthu 2003; Agnani 2013).

There is even more to the picture. For such contradictions and contentions extended from the mutual making, the shared fabrication, of the Enlightenment and the counter-Enlightenment through to the face-offs and admixtures between analytical and hermeneutical procedures (e.g., Kelley 1998; Berlin 2001: 1–24; McMahon 2002; Zammito 2002). These crossovers variously shored up the developmental idea of universal history (Dube 2017a). Here was the constitutive crisscrossing of Hume's querying of an abstract reason, which reveals the formative not-oneness of the Enlightenment, *and* the racial framings integral to the progressivist developmentalism upholding his thought, such that a radical skepticism was yet unable to enter these overwrought recesses (Dube et al. nd). We are in the face of an acute interplay of race and reason, a dynamic that underlay the thought of Kant in overlapping yet distinct ways (Wright nd). As the next chapter discusses, such prior processes of meaning and power underlay the institutionalizations and contentions of anthropology and history as disciplines of modernity from the second half of the nineteenth century and in times and terrains that have come after.

Abiding antinomies between static, traditional communities and dynamic, modern societies have played a crucial role in exactly these scenarios. Three points stand out. First, underlying the disciplinary formations of anthropology and history, the broad binary alluded to above has articulated other enduring oppositions between ritual and rationality, myth and history, community and state, magic and the modern, East and West, and emotion and reason. Second, as salient imprints of developmental-temporal projections of universal-natural history as well as singular-spatial pathways of an exclusive-Western modernity such antinomian procedures and oppositions have not only sought to name and describe but to objectify and reshape the subjects of their desire and despair, a point that was noted above. Third, the actual elaborations of the pervasive separations between enchanted/ traditional cultures and disenchanted/modern societies have imbued them with contradictory value and contrary salience, including ambivalences, ambiguities, and excesses of authority and alterity. These contending attributes simultaneously straddle rationalist and historicist, progressivist and romantic, and analytical and hermeneutical dispositions; post-Enlightenment thought and non-Western scholarship; and the actions and apprehensions of subjects of modernity, at large.[11] All this suggests that anthropological and historical knowledges, far from being easily autonomous academic enquiries, emerge densely embedded in the world, that is as *worlded*. They are, in a word, disciplines of modernity.

The idea of modern knowledges as disciplinary practices itself is not new.[12] At the same time, the importance of disciplinary knowledges – beginning at the end of the eighteenth century and acquiring momentum from the mid-nineteenth century – had come about without the frequent use of the term discipline as such.[13] Indeed, it is from the second half of 1910s through the latter part of 1960s that "disciplinarity" together with "autonomy" came to be clearly named, celebrated, and sedimented in academic practice (Forman 2012). Taken together, the issue that reaches out for discussion is the emergence since the nineteenth century of institutionalized enquiries in the human sciences as producing and probing modernity, not simply as conceptual construct but as material formation. At stake are a range of key questions, urgent enough to be raised here but that I defer for discussion later (especially in Dube et al. nd.)

Considering the dominant branches of the social sciences, in what ways did the three-fold bourgeois separation of key human activity into the domains of the market, the state, and society now come to be mirrored in the tripartite disciplinary division of economics, political science, and sociology? Were such connections principally instrumental (e.g., Wallerstein 1996)? Which were the various worldly and occult influences shaping these nomothetic enquiries – as well as anthropology cast in an evolutionist guise – in comparison to those of more hermeneutic and romanticist dispositions? What are the limits to approaching these knowledges principally via histories of ideas, filiations of concepts, or even intellectual history? Are they not better understood together as disciplines of modernity, forces of worlding, and lineaments of authority that have variously formed and transformed the global and the planetary, the human and the more-than-human? In what distinct ways do these enquiries appear bearing the impress of empire and nation, capital and class, racial hierarchies and gendered inequities – their construal and critique? How are we to explore the differences across disciplines in their mechanisms of world-ing, from economics and development (e.g., Polanyi 1944; Escobar 2011; Mitchell 2002; Tellmann 2017; see also, Ferguson 1990; Hill and Myatt 2010) through to international relations and political science (Shankaran 2021; Shilliam 2021)? Indeed, in what ways have the disciplines in turn been world-ed? From the "scandal of Western domi-nation" (Fabian 1983) through to the enduring alterities sown in and out of anthropological enquiry (Comaroff and Comaroff 1992, 2009; Lutz and Collins 1993; Pemberton 1994; di Leonardo 2000)? And, con-cerning history, from the mutual begetting of nationalist imaginaries and historical narratives to the developmentalist family-romance of civilization and progress?

After disciplines, what of archives? Actually, my emphases put a ques-tion mark on archives as stable, certified, and warrantied (re)sources of authority, knowledge, and history. Indeed, the querying of the cer-tainty of the archive – questionings of guarantees that turned archival research into a disciplinary fetish for the historian (much as fieldwork became a totemic ritual for the anthropologist) – has pointed toward other possibilities. Underscored forthwith have been the requirements of reconfiguring archives as contradictory and contended, discipli-nary and open-ended, anxious and emergent undertakings of power and meaning, command and erasure, inscription and rewriting. This means accessing but also exceeding abstract structures of argument concerning the archive as commencement and commandment, private psyche and public access (alongside their spatial vacillations), mem-ory and forgetting, past and future (Derrida 1996; see also, Ketelaar 2001) and of the archive "as first the law of what can be said, the sys-tem which governs the appearance of statements as unique events" (Foucault 1972: 129), in order to uncover the discursive rules govern-ing the distinct epistemes of knowledge-formations (Foucault 1970). It equally intimates the importance of thinking through the ways in which archives sanctify and sacrifice, bury and disinter, exorcize and exhume pasts and histories (Hamilton et al. 2002; Hartman 2008; Fuentes 2016; see also, Morgan 2021). For at stake are bids of "seeing *with* the archive" (Ketelaar 2001: 135, emphasis in the original), at once cautiously "against" (for example, Guha 1983) yet critically "along" (Stoler 2008; see also Ginzburg 1985) the archival grain, attempt-ing to unravel "tacit narratives of knowledge and power" (Ketelaar 2001: 135) but ever eschewing simple celebrations of the work of coun-ter-archives, counter-memories, and counter-histories as embodying unsullied alterity, resistance, and difference.[14]

All this has large implications. These extend from the presence of anthropologies and histories – as part of the human sciences – through to the place of philosophical and scientific thought as archives inscribing the disciplines and subjects of modernity, their traces and tracks. If such heterogenous archives demand particular procedures of reading, distinct protocols of deciphering, the issues I have outlined equally interrogate the *a priori* boundary between the archive and the field, the putatively discrete loci of anthropological and historical thought. Specifically, all of this reaches beyond projections and politics of archives-as-usual. Made possible now is a re-visitation of ethnographic writing and anthropological assumption as an archive of modernity, constitutive of its disciplines, including in considerations of Dalit "religions." Indeed, together with recent historical writing, such repositories underscore the importance of exploring the broader nature of caste and power when viewed from Dalit experiences and apprehensions (Chapter 3). At the same time, they no less allow for constructions of a historical anthropology of entitlement and affect in the plutocratic present. Such endeavor turns upon the distinct construal of an emergent archive as well as forms of critical description, which interleave ethnographic vignettes, analytical emphases, and anecdotal theory (Chapter 4). At the end, bringing home such considerations, the work engages with even wider traditions of philosophical thought and social-political theory, also approaching these as an archive, drawing upon their insights and blind-sights. Here are to be found explorations of earthly immanence and the querying of worldly-scholastic transcendence, not in relation to the divine but in terms of the cultural privilege and the modern scholasticisms of everyday academic arenas (Chapter 5).

Taken together, the book proffers distinct ways of articulating anthropology and history as necessarily-split disciplines and archives of modernity – in their formation, elaboration, and transformation. Needless to say, such renderings of archives and disciplines, as concept and practice, prudently elaborate their contentions, contradictions, and contingencies. This is also evident in the manner in which eschewing familiar analytical separations – easily-accessed and pervasively-present – this book brings together Dalits and elites, affect and entitlement, quotidian domains and academic terrains, anthropological objects and scholarly subjects, and worldly immanence and modern scholasticism as mutual fields of understanding and description. It is such critical imaginaries and searching juxtapositions that sustain the distinctive emphases of *Disciplines of Modernity*, its exact interweaving of narrative and theory.

Unfolding Arguments

We have noted that in discussing together history and anthropology, the two are principally framed as already-known, taken-for-granted knowledges. Unsurprisingly, accounts of the mutual dialogues of these enquiries often assume "presentist" and "parochial" attributes. In contrast, as a salient segment of the wider work, Chapter 2 articulates anthropology and history as disciplines and archives of modernity – in their making and unmaking. At stake indeed are critical juxtapositions that sieve these enquiries against and along the grain of their formidable conceits, attending to their constitutive oppositions and assumptions. On the one hand, the chapter explores the formative connections of historical and anthropological knowledges with the Enlightenment and Romanticism, race and reason, empire and nation, hermeneutic and analytical procedures, and their incessant interplay. On the other hand, it critically yet cautiously explores the terms and textures of culture and power, tradition and modernity, and time and space. It does this by following the salient intersections of history and anthropology with a range of critical understandings, from post-foundational and postcolonial perspectives to considerations of gender and sexuality onto subaltern and decolonial frames. This brings to the fore newer understandings of colony and nation, empire and modernity, state and sexuality, histories and heritage(s), alterity and gender. At the same time, in taking up these tasks, throughout the endeavor, there is no losing sight of that original opposition between the "savage/native" and the "civilized/modern" for disciplines of modernity.

Taking forward such emphases, Chapter 3 thinks through earlier ethnographic writing as a modern "archive" in order to revisit Dalit "religions." It explores the nature of power in the caste order when viewed from Dalit positions and perspectives; the historical constitution of caste under empire by drawing on recent scholarship; the terms at once of the Dalit's critical exclusion from and their unequal inclusion in caste domains; the varied responses of Dalits to hierarchy and authority in quotidian terrains; and, finally, the intimate interleaving of politics and religions, in their widest senses. On offer are lineaments of anthropological practice as offering archival traces and disciplinary tracks of modernity, its oppositions and elisions, turning on the "native" and the "modern."

Following the book's discussion of Dalits, Chapter 4 critically considers elites and entitlements. It offers fragments of a historical anthropology of privilege and prerogative, as bound to capital and class as well as gender and alterity – in neoliberal and nationalist times, under plutocratic and populist temporalities. The study started as an ethnography and history of my high school cohort, the class of 1979, of Modern School in New Delhi. Gradually, the exercise has moved onto draw in power-brokers, hedge-fund managers, investment bankers, and crony capitalists as well as journalists, bureaucrats, publicists, lawyers, artists, and academics. Amidst distinct approaches to such subjects, the chapter offers an exploratory excursus into life-worlds of entitlement and affect, memory and privilege, and capital and friendship. The wider historical stage for the endeavor is the movement from statist developmentalism to neoliberal nationalism in the political economy of India from the mid-1970s through to the present. At stake is a critical-descriptive bid that interleaves and layers ethnographic vignettes, everyday tales, sociological snapshots, analytical emphases, and anecdotal theory – all the while attending to the habitations of archives of our own making.

Finally, in tenor with the rest of the book, its closing chapter no less eschews the exceptionalisms that abound in the academy. In their stead, it enters into the protocols of salient traditions of philosophical thought and social-political theory, which are again approached as a particular archive. Specifically, I consider here issues of earthly immanence and worldly-scholastic transcendence by focusing on modern scholasticism. Such scholasticisms intimate pervasive procedures that turn their particular case into the general story while forgetting the conditions that make this possible. It is exactly such spectacular conjuring that the essay refers to as worldly-scholastic transcendence: implicit assumptions of immaculate knowledge that occlude and ignore the traces and tracks of its maculate birth on this planet. Against this is contrasted the presence of earthly immanence, which militates against routine assumptions of the disenchantment of – and detachment toward – the world. Seizing upon such earthly immanence, the chapter critically explores how modern scholasticism and worldly transcendence formidably beget and betoken the cultural privilege of academic arenas, embodied at once in the latter's conceptual conventions as well as their everyday life-worlds.

Coda

As we reach the end of this introductory excursus, what are the directions that a reading of *Disciplines of Modernity* might point toward? First, to explore together history and anthropology suggests the importance of continuing to stay with and think through their presumptions and productivities, complicities and segregations, now exactly as disciplines and archives of modernity. Second, at stake are the acute limits of readily splitting apart the knowing subject from its object of enquiry, in order instead to consider them conjointly, even uneasily, by tracking their mutual illuminations and interrogations of each other, the ways in which these knowledges/practices come together and fall apart. Third, I keep in view here future genealogies of ethnographic, historical, and other accounts of emergent worlds, made and unmade by precarities and pandemics, the nonhuman and the Anthropocene. In such accounts and their genealogies, analytical optics, objects of knowledges, and knowing subjects could usefully inhabit shared frames and common fields, holding up mutual mirrors to each other.[15] Fourth and finally, all of this suggests ethically eschewing pervasive performances in academic arenas of the novelty of the author's analyses. Ahead of the "contemporary arrogance" that celebrates the "uniqueness" of our own knowledges and times (Trouillot 2010: 46), it is important to be vigilant rather of the burdens of the past, the paradoxes of the present, the contents of posterity. It is in these ways that we could better respond to the probing, quotidian questions that are said to have punctuated Maurice Merleau-Ponty's seminars: "Where are we? What time is it?"

Notes

1 Having variously learned from many of these tendencies, it is yet important to ask critical questions, especially in the spirit of unraveling problems *and* possibilities. In this light, how might we approach the shared assumptions of intellectual transcendence of "hegemonic liberal-rational thought" and its "radical subaltern critique," especially as articulated by race, caste, and subaltern studies? Considering my debt to feminist understandings, I now bring up some more of the same. Here, Donna Haraway's (1990) insistence on conjoining rather than resolving contradictions in feminist theory, when approached side by side with Joan Scott's (1996) articulations of "only paradoxes to offer" in elaborations of feminist history, have pointed me toward the need to stay with and think through critical tensions, conceptual and quotidian – in a spirit of earthly immanence rather than the will to worldly-scholastic transcendence, a hybrid term that shall be discussed in Chapter 4. Together with the writings of many, many other scholars, all of this suggests also of course the requirements of ever confronting how the scholars' pervasive *ought* repeatedly stands-in for social worlds and their murkiness, remaking these in the image of *our* own analytics and inclinations, yet often side-stepping the compelling claims of strange dreams and uneven desires.
2 Elsewhere (Dube 2004a, 2010, 2017a, 2019a) I have elaborated such emphases in dialogue with a wide body of critical literature, which I cannot return to here.

3 Later on in this Introduction – as in the book – I turn to broad implications of the opposition between power and difference, authority and alterity, as bound to pervasive antinomian idealizations that characterize disciplines and archives of modernity.

4 This can also mean holding up a mirror to the assumption, including hubris, of salient and supple scholarship, turning on different strands of "connected," "global," and "global-intellectual" histories and as well as "early," "alternative," and "multiple" modernities. (These tendencies have much to teach us of course, but by principally reading them with a critical and open eye.) For procedures querying the scholarly strains mentioned above see Aldeman 2017; Dube 2017a: 83–84; Banerjee 2020: 4–5; and 2011: 262–274).

5 Two further points. On the one hand, appreciative of my methodological move to extend a mutual hermeneutic toward understanding privilege and prerogative (Chapter 4) *and* exploring marginalization and exclusion (Chapter 3), Prathama Banerjee has importantly asked: How are we to conceptualize the difference between caste-race-class dominance and academic-institutional-scholastic elitism? Desisting from the temptations to readily separate these formations or to uneasily fold them one into another, let me turn elliptically instead to Donna Haraway's (1990) "cyborg metaphor" and her "informatics of domination." Here, the detailing by Haraway of the deep entrenchment of women in networked hegemony suggests the importance of turning her insights to the constitutive embedding yet contending unraveling of academic arenas within social hierarchies. At the same time, such moves are crucially supplemented by Sande Cohen's (1986) discussion of historical cultures as variously complicit upon wider matrices of power, an insight that finds ever newer meanings in the neoliberal University, especially its inclinations and incitements toward exclusion and expertise, identity and identification. Here, the immensely productive challenges and contentions of Race and Native – as well as Dalit and Adivasi – studies need to be approached alongside their emphatically poignant complicities and contradictions. At stake is the mediation of higher education by the structures and strictures – and the circuit and circus – of capital and nation (see especially, Simpson and Smith 2014; Simpson 2020). On the other hand, given the manner in which much of my work straddles the everyday and the academic, an acknowledgment is essential. It was my strange, affective meetings with Sara Ahmed, Sarah Franklin, and Dolly the Sheep (Franklin 2007), amidst a curious conference founded on extraordinary entitlements of family wealth of Brazilian rubber-barons, which acutely underlined to me the requirements of reigning in our "ought" – in work as in life. Issues of affect are discussed ahead.

6 In bringing to the center issues of embodiment, I track the affective and the sensuous as constitutive of the corporeality of reason(s) as well as reason(s) of corporeality. Yet, all of this means further that I do not approach affect as intimating only interiority and sense as principally surface. To query such an inside : outside dichotomy is to track the mutual movements of experience and reason – their formations and transformations – without readily collapsing the one into the other. All of this of course bears greater discussion, which I cannot offer here.

7 The last point assumes importance in view of the varieties of emphases on experience, embodiment, and emotion – intimating the dense materiality of being, the ontological immediacy of life – in studies of gender and race, the indigenous and the Dalit. Having learned much from several of these studies, my difference lies with those that proclaim somewhat singular critical exceptions for their own life-worlds ahead of the exclusive premises of disenchanted knowledges, overweening analytics, and disaffected reasons, all composite of dominant dystopias. In speaking of each world and all worlds, human and non-human, as being corporeal and sensuous, affective and embodied is not to proclaim their *sameness* as a universal utopia. It is to recognize rather their *difference* – existential and ethical, epistemic and ontological – as borne of contending relationships, contentious entanglements, and contradictory processes, already across history and ever in the here-and-now. My reference is to shifting formations of meaning and mastery, anxiety and authority, dissonance and desire, exclusion and hierarchy, sociality and power, signaling issues to be addressed in a co-authored book (Dube et al. nd). See also, Chapter 3.

8 Both here and in Chapter 5, concerning immanence I have sought to bring together a range of different arguments derived from distinct traditions of understanding. The overlaps and tension between their assumptions and emphases require further staying with, critical thinking through, which I cannot pursue in this book.

9 To the unsuspecting reader, I am suggesting that the Janus-faced nature of modernity, its decisive split-ness, is made up of processes that are enmeshed with each other. Dispensing at once with heroic histories and dystopian totalities, at stake are recognitions and requirements of checkered narratives. Thus, modernity is made up of formative conjunctions between: the Renaissance and mercantilism; "the Age of Discovery" and deaths by genocide; births of democracy and expropriations of settler-colonialisms; reason and race; science and slavery; industry and colony; technologies and traditions; Enlightenment and empire; secularized religion(s) and seductions of state; figures of disenchantment and enchantments of modernity; liberty and gender; egalitarian spirits and hetero-normative assumption; and critical theory and modern scholasticism. These are only a few examples, taken from my wider discussions of such questions (Dube 2017a, 2019a, 2020b).

10 Here, my reference is to historical actors who have been both *subject to* the processes of power and meanings of modernity, but also exactly *subjects shaping* these procedures. That is, the two meanings of the term subject. Widening the address of modernity, the subjects who have fashioned while being subordinated to its processes include indigenous nations/communities, the bearers of blackness (at "home" and in "diasporas"), and other subaltern and marginal – peasant, artisan, working-class, migrant, destitute – peoples, all of different sexualities across the world. Needless to say, such subjects have diversely articulated (gendered and sexualized) modern processes of colony and post-colony, empire and nation, and slavery and settler-colonialism. Accompanied by middle-class and elite actors, all these subjects have registered within their measures and meanings the formative contradictions, contentions, and contingencies of modernity in non-Western and Western theatres. On these questions,

including the distinctions and overlaps between modern subjects and subjects of modernity, see Dube (2004a, 2010, 2011, 2017a; and Dube and Banerjee-Dube 2019).

11 Once more, I have elaborated elsewhere these emphases, in close conversations with wider literatures, especially in Dube (2017a).

12 On the one hand, Michel Foucault (1967, 1979) long ago linked the new enquiries in the human sciences of the eighteenth century as disciplinary mechanisms to define and control subjects of modernity. Indeed, the emergent *medico-juridical complex* conjoined disciplinary enquiry with bureaucratic innovation in its "therapeutic" and "rehabilitative" subject-constitution. On the other hand, considering political economy, ahead of Adam Smith and alongside John Locke, the progenitors of modern demography, John Graunt and William Petty, were "thinking through problems of population and mobility at precisely the moment when England had solidified its commitment to the slave trade," underlying the conjoint construal of economic value and hierarchical classification, slave economics and racial capitalism, and gendered labor and commodified kinship (Morgan 2021).

13 All of this entails intriguing genealogies of the term discipline and its usages. These include the overlaps and distinctions of discipline in relation to "profession," "self-discipline," and "disciplining" (of children, for example), ably discussed by Paul Forman (2012).

14 At issue are much more than terms of conceptual refinement and empirical finesse. Colin Koopman (2010) focuses on the work of Foucault as arguing that reason and madness as well as power and autonomy/freedom require understanding as "reciprocally incompatible" categories. Here, I would like to suggest that the "couples" of madness and rationality and freedom (or autonomy) and power need to be read together with two other sets of copulas under regimes of modernity. For one part, the "foundational" idealized oppositions between ritual and rationality, myth and history, community and state, magic and the modern, East and West, and emotion and reason; and for another, the "post-foundational" – or at least, post-foundationally inflected – splits between power and difference, authority and alterity. Are at stake perhaps constitutively reciprocal yet already incompatible copulas of a foundational and post-foundational provenance that compel relentless purification? I take up such questions in Dube et al. (n.d.)

15 For distinct expressions of the shapes that such procedures might take see, for instance, Li (2020) and Mazzarella (2017). See also, Banerjee (2020) and Jobson (2020); and contrast, Povinelli (2016) and Gold (2017). We have much to learn from all these distinct endeavors.

2 Rethinking Disciplines
Anthropology and History

In discussing together history and anthropology, it is often acknowledged that the relationship between the two has been contradictory and contentious but their interplay has also been prescient and productive. At the same time, such considerations, turning on dissension and dialogue, are principally premised upon framing anthropology and history as already-known, taken-for-granted knowledges. Here, each prefigured enquiry is seen as characterized by its own discrete desires and distinct methods, concerning research and writing, analysis and description. If these entities are presumed as being or becoming complete unto themselves, this means too that accounts of disciplinary dialogues equally acquire palpably "presentist" and "parochial" characteristics. Arguably, what is required is a different disposition – the lineaments of which already, actually exist – to the subjects of history and anthropology, their tensions and intersections, their contentions and crossovers. As the Introduction has discussed in detail, this means approaching and unraveling anthropology and history as disciplines of modernity.

Overture: Convergent Questions

In such re-visitation, at least three matters assume salience. First, to juxtapose anthropology and history is to rethink these enquiries, sieving them against and along their formidable conceits.[1] Second, such tasks require exploring the constitutive linkages of the two with the wider processes of meaning and power of the Enlightenment and Romanticism, empire and nation, race and reason, and hermeneutic and analytical procedures, as well as with broader transformations of the human sciences. These reveal curious connections as much as mutual makeovers, especially when mapped as careful genealogies and critical poetics of anthropological and historical knowledges as well as

DOI: 10.4324/9781003347569-2

their conjunctions. Third and finally, at stake are bids that stay with and think through received configurations of culture and power, the traditional and the modern, and space and time based on the shared sensibilities of anthropology, history, and orientations such as post-structuralist and postcolonial perspectives, decolonial and subaltern studies. All of this makes possible the tracking of incisive articulations, empirical and theoretical, of subaltern formations and historical conceptions, colonial cultures and imperial imperatives, gender and sexuality, nation and state, slavery and heritage, and alterity and modernity on the cusp of anthropology and history as well as their larger intersections with the human sciences.

Now, if the imagination and writing of history are often traced back to classical antiquity and its pasts (Kelley 1998), a similar claim can be made about the pursuit and practice of anthropology (Hartog 1988). At the same time, this chapter charts a different course. To start off, I consider the common grounds and key attributes of anthropology and history as institutionalized enquiries formed in the second half of the nineteenth century. Yet I do so only while looking back over my shoulder to delineate prior intellectual-political currents going back to the Enlightenment, Romanticism, and their byways, which have continued to shape later terrains. This sets the stage for the discussion in the chapter of the elaborations and articulations of anthropology and history from the twentieth century onward.

In taking such steps, I stay away from singular readings, grounded in the present, that plot the pasts of the discipline – including their meetings, mating(s), and makeovers – in tendentious and teleological ways.² Actually, such eschewal on my part is itself premised upon a deciphering of texts and times by attending to their terms and textures. That is, readings and renderings which contextually construe continuities and contradictions, ambivalences and excesses. Taken together, such measures can hopefully unravel a few of the consequences of critically juxtaposing anthropology and history as disciplines of modernity: from their mutual presumptions to their particular distinctions to their contending conjunctions – not as a straight line but as crisscrossing pathways.

Enquiries and Disciplines

Arguably, the common grounds of anthropology and history as disciplines of modernity rest upon enduring oppositions between static, traditional groups (that is, "savage" peoples or "native" communities) on the one hand and dynamic, modern societies (that is, "civilized" states or European orders) on the other.[3] Evidently, such a duality and its distillations have undergirded also other antimonies between ritual and rationality, myth and history, community and state, magic and the modern, emotion and reason, and East and West (Lutz 1988; Comaroff and Comaroff 1992; Dube 1998). Finally, the dichotomies have found diverse values and shifting expressions not only in modern enquiries but among the discrete subjects that the distinctions have named, described, and objectified over at least the past three centuries (Comaroff and Comaroff 2009; Dube 2017a). Taken together, as was elaborated earlier, under consideration are contradictory and contended disciplines of modernity, in the widest senses. Here, the aggrandizing and fraught disciplinary formations have turned upon institutionalized enquiries and commonplace understandings – including the ways in which these terrains come together to fall apart – under colony and empire, nation and state, also variously bearing the prior impress of the Enlightenment and its adversaries.

A Contended Enlightenment

It is apposite, then, to begin with the European Enlightenment of the seventeenth and eighteenth centuries and the accompanying processes of the secularization of Judeo-Christian time.[4] Now, instead of an exclusive Enlightenment I am speaking here of rather more plural Enlightenment*s*, not merely on empirical registers but in critical ways. At stake were distinct expressions of universal and natural history alongside contending strains of rationalism in, say, France and of empiricism-skepticism in, for instance, Britain (Stocking 1987; Kelley 1998; Porter 2000); key challenges to analytical procedures through various counter-Enlightenments that shaped the Enlightenment (Berlin 2001, 1–24; McMahon 2002); and procedures of the secularization of Judeo-Christian time as at once an emergent and consequential idea (Fabian 1983) yet a circumscribed and limited process (Becker 1932; Stocking 1987; see also Crapanzano 2000; Moore 2003; Hamann 2016). After all, the Enlightenment, broadly understood, entailed the reordering of philosophy and the remapping of history, the reworking of human reason and the replotting of human nature. At stake was the rethinking – at once philosophical, historical, and anthropological – of "man," "civilization," and "nature," in places where biblical assumption continued to cast its light and shadow.

On the one hand, despite the critical contentions among such schemes, they could nonetheless frequently project – albeit in necessarily different ways – developmental images of universal history.

This is to say that, from the rationalist, progressivist claims of Voltaire and Immanuel Kant through to the contending, historicist frames of Giambattista Vico and Johann Gottfried von Herder, projected forthwith were grand historical designs of civilization and culture, of Europe and nation (Stocking 1987; Kelley 1998: 211–262). On the other hand, the tension-ridden knowledges never simply coalesced together in order to become a uniform Western (or Enlightenment) mentality. Rather, they pointed toward the face-offs between analytical and hermeneutic orientations, between developmental and historicist imaginaries, and between progressivist and romanticist dispositions. At the same time, across such contentions and conjunctions there lay other key consequences, such as the presence and persistence of developmentalist imaginaries leading to racial assumption, which could upbraid the "skepticism" of David Hume and trump the "understanding" of Kant, such that "race equals place, and all other races, like all other places, are inferior to (white) Europeans and Europe" (Michelle M. Wright, nd; Dube et al. nd).

Taken together, the interplay and admixture of these distinct tendencies across the first half of the nineteenth century underlay the institutionalization of anthropological and historical knowledge in that century's second half.[5] Indeed, these wider, contending but overlapping dispositions to human worlds and their knowing have continued to inform ever since the uneven unraveling of anthropology and history as modern enquiries, revealing also the excesses of meaning these disciplines of modernity have been unable to contain.[6]

Evolutionism and After

The sociocultural evolutionism that characterized British anthropology from the 1860s brought together two separate, prior tendencies: "on the one hand, a study of the variety of mankind that that had yet to free itself from the constraints of biblical assumption; and on the other, a study of the progress of civilization for which a positivistic program was already well established" (Stocking 1987: 45). This conjunction itself turned upon the erosion of the intellectual defenses of antievolutionism, the decline of biblical anthropology, and the increasing legitimacy of naturalistic apprehensions of human variety. Now the key question to be explained was that of the development of civilization, especially the unequal participation of different subjects in its inexorable progress. Thus, linear and progressive time formatively entered the core of evolutionary anthropology and its racial assumption (Fabian 1983), frequently shoring up temporal sequences and hierarchical stages between the savage and the civilized. To be sure, Victorian anthropologists betrayed their own differences and distinctions, as becomes clear from considering the predilections and persuasions of Edward Tylor, Herbert Spencer, Henry Maine, and Lewis Morgan. Yet together they purposefully, tendentiously raided – what appeared to them as – the historical past. In these ways was elaborated a vehement episteme of meaning and power through positivistic, naturalistic, and progressivist articulations of the developmental process of civilization and its elisions.

Biblical assumption had distinctly shaped diffusionist ethnology and comparative philology – joined at the hip by the imaginings and implications of the Tower of Babel – in their search for the unity and variation of humankind through the linkages of history, language, customs, and mythology. Not unlike sociocultural evolutionism, the formative presumptions of these orientations were now challenged by the archeological revolution of the 1850s and the rise of the biological evolutionary paradigm (Fabian 1983; Stocking 1987).[7] All this underlay a variety of challenges to sociocultural evolutionism, including those bearing affective resonances of the romanticist tradition – especially of a German provenance – in newer configurations. In the interest of space, I turn to an important critic of evolutionary anthropology.

As the twentieth century dawned, Franz Boas (1974: 35) defined anthropological knowledge as consisting of "the biological history of mankind in all its varieties; linguistics applied to people without written languages; the ethnology of people without historic records; and prehistoric archeology." This was broadly in keeping with wider ethnological assumption, and Boas added to all these enquiries across his career. At the same time, for "Boas, the 'otherness' which is the subject matter of anthropology was to be explained as the product of change of time" (Stocking 1992: 347), an insistence on the diachronic that covered also his unifying definition of the discipline. Before the end of the century, Boas intimated "a neo-ethnological critique of 'the comparative method' of classical evolutionism" (Stocking 1992: 352–353), which insisted upon on specific historical enquiry, detailed linguistic investigation, and grounded physical anthropology. At the same time, the work of Boas is better understood as straddling the dualism between progressivist and romanticist traditions, interweaving universalistic and rationalist orientations with particularistic and emotional dispositions, which is to say as entwining, while being held in contrapuntal tension by, these contending schemes of modern knowledge (Boas 1928; Stocking 1992). All of this had suggested an enquiry that sought to free itself of racial/biological determinism in order to point toward a disciplinary conception of culture as relativistic and pluralistic. Yet, it is not only that Boas' particular turn to the diachronic, the historical, and the temporal signified a pathway mostly ignored by anthropology during most of the twentieth century.[8] It is importantly the case that the intermeshing of progressivism and romanticism, the interleaving of developmentalism and emotionalism, in Boas' thought defines the limits of his break at once with evolutionist assumption, settler-colonial presumption, and national-liberal settlement. His work is complicit in the appropriation of indigenous lives and lands, predicting the immediate decline and eventual decimation of these people – tragically, inevitably.[9] The status of Boas as a revered ancestor of modern anthropology – a father figure that actively endorsed historical enquiry – is befitting. For Franz Boas is an exemplar of anthropology and history as contradictory and contended disciplines of modernity, who described and remade the world in their mirrors.

History and Its Elisions

Turning to history, its professionalization in the second half of the nineteenth century equally expressed connected contradictions and contentions.[10] At stake were discrete claims on the terms and textures of civilization and culture, shaped by the imperatives of class and race, nation and empire. To begin with, important strands of history-writing representing "historicism," especially instituted as a discipline in Germany, bore a double-sided relationship with the ideas and imaginaries of universal human progress. Expressing hermeneutic, historicist, and counter-Enlightenment impulses, such histories acutely articulated notions of culture, tradition, and the *volk* (folk), principally of the nation. They implicitly interrogated thereby the conceits of an aggrandizing reason as well as developmental schemes of philosophical history that these accounts saw as leitmotifs of the Enlightenment. This could allow for broadly relativistic and pluralistic understandings of cultures and nations.

At the same time, classical historicism followed the influence of Leopold von Ranke's avowals of "source criticism," the official archive, and historical narration (as "telling it the way it really was"). Resting also on the lasting legacy of Barthold Georg Niebuhr, it principally reinforced the exclusive designs of singular histories, turning on a decidedly non-cosmopolitan, indeed divisive, nation and its statist power-politics.[11] The documentary dispositions and the philological methods underlying the historicist principle of continuity meant also that most non-European "others" were banished from the canvas of history, discretely animating thereby the antimonies of modernity. In sum, going back to the compelling influence of Johann Gottfried Herder on these traditions, we find at once the possibilities of pluralist and relativist imaginaries *and* the presence of nationalist and racialist presumptions, putting a particular spin as well on hermeneutic dispositions, analytical orientations, and their conjunctions.

Moreover, the elaboration of the discipline elsewhere in the Euro-American world in the nineteenth century meant that history-writing not only bore the flag of the nation but carried the impress of empire. Here, the proximate pasts of dark terrains, mainly colonial territories, frequently appeared as footnotes and appendices to the *Ur*-history of Europe, even as the extending frontiers of the historical imagination in settler spaces orchestrated their primitive subjects through civilizational allegories (Klein 1999; Wolfe 1999).

Finally, modern histories construed in colonized countries and emergent nations were not merely replications of blueprints out of Europe, but instead imbued their accounts with particular protocols of proof and method, truth and philosophy (Deshpande 2007; Thurner 2011; Chakrabarty 2015). But these accounts of the past were also often envisioned in the image of a progressive European civilization, albeit using unto their own purposes the hierarchies and oppositions of Western modernity (Chakrabarty 1992; Cooper 1994: 1519–1526; Sarkar 1997: 30–42; see also Prakash 1994). Does all of this not point to the emergence of institutionalized history-writing, intimately bound to nation and empire, as a contradictory and contended discipline of modernity?

Anthropology, History, Temporality

The institutionalizations and contentions of anthropology and history as modern enquiries emerged after the wider processes of the French and industrial revolutions; as responses to changes in class structures and the revolutions of 1848; and alongside the consolidations of nations and empires. These developments informed also broad streams of social thought from Karl Marx to Émile Durkheim to Max Weber, figures who were to have a significant impact on history and anthropology in the twentieth century. Indeed, the influence of Durkheim was to play a key role in the disciplinary makeovers of both anthropology and history during the interwar years.

At the turn of the twentieth century, the antievolutionary impulse in anthropology was manifest both in the influence of Franz Boas and the implications of diffusionism. Now, the emergence of fieldwork-based "scientific" anthropology, under the auspices of Bronislaw Malinowski and A. R. Radcliffe-Brown, was premised upon a break with the speculative historical procedures of diffusionism, while bearing a more ambiguous relationship with evolutionism. This put a question mark on history as such within the functionalism of Malinowski (1922) and the structural functionalism of Radcliffe-Brown (1952). The contradistinction between the work of anthropology and the labor of history in these paradigms bore the influence of Durkheimian sociology, such that the privileging of "synchrony" over "diachrony" presupposed that social orders were best apprehended in abstraction from their historical transformations (Kuper 1973: 92–109; Eisenstadt 1990: 243–244; Vincent 1990: 155–171; Stocking 1995: 233–441). Here, the disciplinary emphasis on tracking continuity and consensus – to the neglect of change and conflict – in societal arrangements was premised upon sharply distinguishing non-Western cultures presumed to be held in place by myth and ritual from dynamic Western societies thought to be grounded in history and reason.

All of this has wide implications for anthropology at large. Johannes Fabian (1983) has argued that anthropological inquiry has repeatedly construed its analytic object as its constitutive other through measures turning on temporality, such that the ethnographic object stands ever denied the "coevalness of time" with the instant of the anthropologist subject. Here, the historical time-space of the observing modern subjects and their societies – alongside the taken-for-granted objective time of scientific knowledge – emerge as always ahead of the mythic space-time of the observed objects and their traditions; anthropological analytics and narrative techniques project a lasting "ethnographic present"; and change and transformation usually enter native structure in exogenous ways. Such protocols underlie the "savage slot" (Trouillot 1991) and the "native niche" (Dube 2004a) of anthropology that have been formative of the discipline. This is not to deny that such disciplinary schemas have been attended by exceptions and challenges, issues to which I shall return. The point is that beyond the influence of evolutionist understandings on contemporary anthropology (Thomas 1991), at stake are pervasive modern meta-geographies that authoritatively if ambiguously carve up social worlds into enchanted terrains of tradition and disenchanted domains of modernity.

The crisis of classical historicism and the narrowness of history-writing, their preoccupation with politics in the shadow of the nation, meant that from the early twentieth century there were attempts to found the historical discipline on "scientific" principles as well as to redress the hitherto residual role of society and economy in the historian's craft.[12] For our purposes, special importance is occupied by the Annales school of history-writing in France, which in the 1920s made a decisive break with event-based political history. Drawing on sociological considerations, particularly the work of Durkheim, the Annales suggestively, imaginatively opened up the scope and subject of history-writing to draw in processes of society, economy, and culture (e.g., Bloch 1954; Febvre 1973).[13] At the same time, while registering the importance of such departures, it is important also to resist the persistent tendency that casts the Annales as initiating a gradual expansion of social-cultural history that led inexorably to its eventual embrace of anthropology. Here, we need to consider what was foreclosed by the formative "structural histories" of the Annales as well as to probe the implicit oppositions in their writings between "backward" communities and "civilized" societies, which return us to the common antinomies and mutual hierarchies concerning time and space that link anthropology and history as modern enquiries.[14]

Meanwhile, the simultaneous presence of progressivist and romanticist tendencies in the modern human sciences, meant that imaginative endeavors could critically engage dominant disciplinary designs yet also emerge as constrained by the meta-geographies of modernity. Consider the work of the anthropologist E. E. Evans-Pritchard (1939, 1940) on time and space. Here, the entwining of hermeneutic impulses and analytical tendencies imbue – with their motive force *and* their critical limitations – Evans-Pritchard's considerations of time-space among the Nuer peoples. His hermeneutic renderings unravel the production of time-space among the Nuer within their routine, concrete, and everyday activities, thereby founding the temporal and the spatial in the image of social diversity and cultural heterogeneity. At the same time, simultaneously, following Evans-Pritchard's analytic assertion, the Nuer peoples entirely lack long-term time, revealing lasting projections of non-Western primitive places and Western modern spaces (Munn 1992: 94–98; Dube 2007a: 13–15).

Other Emergences

Evans-Pritchard's exemplary study bears linkages with the wider rethinking of the principal predication of social action on sociological structure within functionalist and structural-functionalist paradigms. Did not the counter-colonial movements, nationalist struggles, and other practices of colonized subalterns during the interwar years reveal a certain discrepancy between classical functionalist apprehensions of social action and the emphatic agency of non-Western subjects? There were diverse shifts within British anthropology after the 1930s: from the efforts of the Rhodes Livingstone Institute in Africa to move the locus of ethnographic enquiry to proletarians (Kuper 1973: 133–135; Vincent 1990: 276–283; Ferguson 1999); through to the emergent interrogation of functionalism within British anthropology, especially its Manchester mutations, which explored anew social conflict, individual action, and collective processes, particularly from the 1950s (Leach 1954; Bailey 1957, 1969; Turner 1957; Barth 1959; Uberoi 1962; Gluckman 1963; see also Worsley 1957). Such efforts could not simply shake off the long shadow cast by functionalist schemes, but they were also not innately opposed to the work being undertaken by social historians at the time. Indeed, here were attempts to think through the autonomy of analytical traditions, which could include wider reconsiderations of disciplines.[15] The last included Evans-Pritchard's (1962: 1–157; see also 1965) famous endorsement of anthropology as a humanistic enquiry as well as his assertions of the intersections between anthropology with history (Evans-Pritchard 1961; see also Schapera 1962). We are in the face of varied endeavors to grapple with the shifting contexts of anthropology; to respond to wider political and historical transformations affecting the discipline and its subjects; and to extend received disciplinary blueprints.

Such bids also characterized anthropology in the United States after World War II. Here, at least three tendencies emphasized the significance of diachronic and historical understandings for the discipline. In the first place, focusing on complex civilizations and social change, the studies of Robert Redfield elaborated continuums of "little" and "great" traditions and communities. His formulations pointed to societal transformations, influenced by forces that were exogenous and endogenous, while understanding anthropology as bridging the breach between historical and scientific enquiry (Redfield 1956). Moreover, shaped by Marxist understandings and leftist politics, the work of anthropologists such as Eric Wolf (1959) and Sydney Mintz (1960) articulated temporal and historical considerations in explorations of political economy, subordinate groups, and political transformations. Finally, the field of "ethnohistory," delineated in the 1950s, came to distinctly combine history and anthropology with limitations and possibilities (Krech 1991).[16]

If at stake were the critical contentions of anthropology as a discipline of modernity, it is also the case that the terms of the temporal remained principally at a remove from the textures of the discipline and its varied specializations. Unsurprisingly, culture was presented principally as a coherent and bounded entity, autonomous from power relations and societal transformations, and relentlessly inward-looking as it turned upon its own axes. Unsurprisingly, even influential work, such as that of Clifford Geertz (1973), which opened up possibilities for anthropology and history by stressing signifying action within webs of meanings tended to remove temporality from the terms of practice within culture (Munn 1992: 98–100; Ortner 1999: 3). This included those later writings where Geertz (1980) turned to cultural pasts.

Disciplinary Transformations

The long 1960s witnessed civil rights, anti-imperialist, radical-student, emergent feminist, and continuing anticolonial endeavors across the world. Did not such processes implicitly indicate the discrepancies between anthropological projections of invariant structures and unchanging cultures, on the one hand, and emphatic assertions of human action and history-making in wider worlds (Comaroff 1985; Lan 1985; but consider also sociological accounts of peasant movements in the 1970s), on the other? Of course, such reminders of the urgent practices of historical subjects often escaped disciplinary attention. Yet they were constitutive for the emerging critiques of the social sciences, at large, extending from what Fabian (1983: x) was later to call the "scandal" of Western domination to the place of anthropology in the outrage, including considerations of the discipline's complicity with colonialism (Gough 1968; Banaji 1970; Asad 1973; see also Hymes 1972). None of this is to deny that exactly in these contexts, the success of "dependency" theories and "world-system" analytics – interrogating the capitalist and imperialist continuities of Western domination in non-Western theatres through polarities of core and periphery, development and underdevelopment – entailed a privileging of structure/system that went hand in hand with an undermining of action/practice (Wolfe 1997: 380–420; see also Stoler 1995b: vii–xxxiv). The point might well be that the rhetorical avowal of history and power intimated the transformations of the human sciences that were under way, underscoring their contradictions and contentions as disciplines of modernity.

At stake specially were critical explorations across different enquiries of the interplay between structure and practice, rules and processes, social organization and historical action (Bourdieu 1977; Giddens 1979; Comaroff and Roberts 1981; Abrams 1983; Ortner 1984; see also Williams 1973; Thompson 1978). Although it had antecedents, from the second half of the 1970s an increasing emphasis on practice, process, and power came to characterize anthropological inquiry. The influence of world systems theory and structural Marxist analytics did not simply disappear: but the emergent forms of anthropological practice distinctly attended to the temporal textures of culture and subject, meaning and structure, social reproduction, and societal transformation (Rosaldo 1980; Fabian 1983; Fox 1985; Sahlins 1985; Cohn 1987; Dirks 1987; Ohnuki-Tierney 1987, 1990, 1993; Sider 1986; see also Appadurai 1982). Indeed, history was making urgent claims upon anthropology (Cohn 1980, 1981; Sahlins 1993). Engaging the archival record, important ethnographic writings focused on meanings and practices of non-Western subjects as critical attributes of the contradictory elaboration of colonialism and capitalism, themselves understood as temporally and culturally layered fields, revealing too the sustained interchanges between Western and non-Western worlds (Nash 1979; Taussig 1980, 1985; Price 1983; Comaroff 1985; Stoler 1985).

Underscoring the presence of power and difference in formations of meaning and practice, being questioned were anthropological objects of enquiry as insinuating bounded and coherent entities, based on antinomies between traditional orders and modern societies. Simply put, the conjoint emphases on process, practice, and power went on to reinvigorate the study of such staples of the discipline as religion and ritual, magic and witchcraft, symbolism and law, and kinship and kingship (Kelly and Kaplan 1990; Krech 1991; Merry 1992; Peletz 1995; Reddy 1999).

At the same time, the emergence of an anthropology of Europe from the late 1970s had complementary, compelling consequences: it queried reified distinctions between the West as theory/self and the non-West as object/other; probed *a priori* projections of an exclusive, unique Europe ahead of the plurality of its variously fissured social facts; revisited the imperial, "crypto-colonial," and nationalist genealogies of the discipline; untangled particular constructions of histories and identities on the Continent and its margins; and unraveled the discursive constructs that at once underlie anthropology itself as an ethnographic object and the cultural identifications it studies as theoretical subjects (Herzfeld 1982, 1985, 1987, 1992, 2009; Hastrup 1992; Barrera-González et al. 2017; see also Rabinow 1989; Latour 1993; Asad et al. 1997). Unsurprisingly, these dispositions have all variously involved implicit and explicit recognition that not merely wider social processes but anthropological analyses are themselves enacted temporally as well as spatially.

Fates of Cultures

The changing fate of "culture" – that category of categories in ethnography in its American incarnation yet with implications for
understandings of "structure" and "tradition" concerning anthropology at large – brings home such reconfigurations. For the terms
of culture were now shown to *contain*, within themselves, lineaments
of dominance and contentions of dissonance. That is, projections of
seamless-static cultures excised their arrangements of authority and
alterity – entailing the fissures of community and gender, race and
office, stratification and sexuality – shaped over the last five centuries by colonialism and capitalism, nation and modernity (Sider 1980;
Asad 1983; Rebel 1989).

Unsurprisingly, these critiques of the culture concept were taken
forward in distinct directions in the last quarter of the twentieth
century. From the "reflexive" turn in the "experimental" ethnography of the 1980s that highlighted questions of narrative "authority" in
ethnographic "representation" (Marcus and Cushman 1982; Clifford
and Marcus 1986; Marcus and Fischer 1986) through to interrogations
of anthropology as itself an alterity-engendering mechanism that has
exoticized and institutionalized cultural difference unto its particular disciplinary ends (Lutz and Collins 1993; di Leonardo 2000) and
made culture stick to particular locales (Marcus 1997; Abu-Lughod
1999). And from demands for writing against culture on account of
its complicities with dominant projects of empire, nation, and globalization (Pemberton 1994) through to the articulations of culture
as interwoven with transnational processes of diaspora and modernity, entangled identities, and hybrid histories (Foster 1991; Merry
1992; Alonso 1994; Hefner 1998; van der Veer 2001). Unsurprisingly,
it has become evident also that rather more than simply an analytical
device, culture is a concept-entity and a critical resource that has been
central to the imaginings and practices of the very people the notion
has variously sought to define and describe: from the fourth world to
the first world; from impoverished indigenous peoples to privileged
ethnic constituencies; from violent religious militants to dominant
stake-holders of power.

Needless to say, these critiques and such emphases have neither been
all of a piece nor have all turned toward history: but they have nonetheless variously emphasized the salience of practice, process, and power
as constitutive of social worlds and their scholarly apperceptions.
Unsurprisingly, these emphases have followed upon wider historical developments: the end of innocence of the Bandung Era as newly

independent nations revealed their authoritarian and corrupt designs; the retreat of the institutionalized visions of state-sponsored equality with the fall of the Berlin Wall; the rise and decline of the magic of unfettered capital and the Midas of the market; and the ascent to power in the second decade of the twenty-first century of plutocratic and populist regimes that avow entitlement, while raising walls of different descriptions.

Affective Histories

Meanwhile, the gradual expansion after World War II of the discipline of history – not unlike that of anthropology – included an increase in professional specialization and job opportunities. If these shored up the development of identifiable terrains of social history, the wider historical developments after World War II have had their own impact on the discipline at large. For our purposes, the elaboration of important trends in social/cultural history beginning in the 1950s might be usefully understood as part of common attempts with different emphases to construe accounts that focused on subjects hitherto marginalized from the historical record, including the wider democratization of history-writing (Dube 2004a: 133–137). The influence of anticolonial imaginaries and the Soviet invasion of Hungary, the civil rights movement and the reckoning with Nazi pasts, the energies of 1968 and the mobilizations against the Vietnam War all played a role here. Considering the paucity and perversity of the historical record of marginal subjects, here were bids to seek out distinct archival materials, read them with new eyes, and think anew their validities as "sources" of history, all of which equally resulted in dialogues with anthropology (Thomas 1963, 1971; Thompson 1972, 1977; Sewell 1980) but also conversations with other disciplines, including sociology, demography, and psychology, further leading historical narratives in fresh directions.

The new forms of historiography carried critical possibilities but also their own limitations. I have in mind major traditions that have included the third generation (and after) of the Annales school in France (e.g., Ladurie 1979; Le Goff 1980; Schmitt 1983; Chartier 1993); the erstwhile British Communist Group of Historians (e.g., Hill 1973; Hobsbawm 1993; Thompson 1993); historians of African American slavery in North America (Genovese 1974; Levine 1977); the collective subaltern studies project focusing on South Asia (e.g., Guha 1982–1989; Chatterjee and Pandey 1992; Arnold and Hardiman 1994; Amin and Chakrabarty 1996; see also Dube 2004a:

129–163); pioneering social-cultural histories of Europe also of a North American provenance (Davis 1977; Sewell 1980; Darnton 1985; see also Scott 1988); "microhistory" in Italy (Ginzburg 1980; Levi 1988; Muir and Ruggiero 1991); and "Alltagsgeschichte"– the "history of everyday life"– in Germany (Medick and Sabean 1984; Sabean 1984, 1990; Lüdtke 1995).

Rather than tracking these tendencies in a "whiggish" manner as necessarily, increasingly opening out to anthropology, it might be more useful to ask questions of their possibilities and problems: that is, the ways these tendencies principally extended the terms of the dominant disciplinary coupling of history and nation under regimes of modernity; and at the same time, how these departures were also unable to break with such lasting bonds, to escape their long shadows, readily, easily (Dube 2017a: 128–130). The productive ambiguities of these traditions have been followed by an even wider opening of new cultural histories, which is evident from accounts that think through prior tensions while asking and addressing newer questions (Scott 1996; Sabean 1998; Schmitt 1998; Eley 2005; Sewell 2005).[17] Yet, as we shall see, such recent accounts and their own assumption are themselves being shifted and undone through even newer narratives, especially within the terms and textures of our times. Actually, under issue once more are the contentions and contradictions of history and historiography as disciplines of modernity.

Critical Concurrences

Keeping this in view, I turn now to the shared renovations and mutual entailments of anthropology and history over the past four decades. Such makeovers have been severally influenced by various emergences. I have in mind the shifting political contexts of the last four decades; the "linguistic" and "cultural" – alongside the "ontological" and "affective" – turns and twists in the human sciences; the key crossovers of historical and anthropological enquiry with anti- and postfoundational understandings; and their acute interchanges with postcolonial perspectives and subaltern studies.[18] Together, on offer have been imaginative interrogations of abiding antinomies of modern disciplines; of lasting legacies of historical progress; and of persistent projections of an imaginary Europe and a reified West as modernity, history, and destiny for the world at large (Dube 2017a).

Now, in these terrains, archival readings and critical fieldwork have at once supported and probed each other. This has queried too the fetish of the field and the purity of the archive in order to rethink anthropology and history. All told, more useful than segregating disciplines is to track their entangled energies in the conjoint elaborations of specific themes, particular questions. Such concerns and issues extend across key endeavors announcing the contemporary confluence of historical anthropology, ethnographic history, and cultural history.

Subalterns and Margins

The newer emphases of historical-anthropological accounts – alongside the influence of critical histories of subordinate groups, including subaltern studies – underlie astute explorations of the identities and endeavors, consciousness and practices, and meanings and persuasions of subaltern peoples and marginal communities, straddling their configurations and transformations, particularly in non-Western arenas. Far from durable depictions of "people without history" (Wolf 1982) – insinuating anachronistic customs, compulsive consensus, and "never-never" traditions (Cohn 1980) – such subjects have appeared as active participants in wider processes turning on identities and histories, colonialisms and empires, nation and nationalisms, states and citizens, and modernity and globalization. Here are to be found players and protagonists that imbue such procedures with distinct perceptions and practices, temporalities and spatialities, and terms and textures.

On the one hand, the constitutive location of subaltern formations within wide-ranging processes of power and meaning includes as well their own internal divisions as expressed in terms of property, gender, law, and office. On the other hand, the layered negotiations and various contestations, especially in religious-ritual political idioms, issued by subordinate groups toward dominant processes – of empire and nation, state and capital, war and violence – reveal acute intersections between authority, action, and alterity. Unsurprisingly, these twin emphases have been often unraveled together in accounts sustained by the interplay between anthropology and history (Ileto 1979; Rosaldo 1980; Taussig 1980, 1985; Guha 1983; Price 1983; Comaroff 1985; Lan 1985; Stoler 1985; Sider 1986; Hardiman 1987; Gutiérrez 1991; Kelly 1991; Amin 1995; Kaplan 1995; Mayaram 1997; Dube 1998; Skaria 1999; Mallon 2005; Pandian 2009; Rao 2009; Subramanian 2009; see also Das 1995; Kasturi 2002).

History and Pasts

It only follows that the critical rethinking of history-writing and historical consciousness – including representations of the past and contentions of temporality – has come to lie at the core of newer scholarship. There has been an emphasis on the socio-spatial plurality of cultural pasts, the manner in which history and temporality are distinctly apprehended and severally enacted by particular social groups (Rosaldo 1980; Price 1983, 1990; Hill 1988; Cohen and Atieno Odhiambo 1989; Rappaport 1994; Amin 1995; Florida 1995; Dube 1998; Skaria 1999; White 2000; Banerjee-Dube 2007). Such multiple enactments and constructions of history have featured not only local voices (Hastrup 1992; Shyrock 1997) but nonverbal expressions of dance and music (McCall 2000) as well as nonhuman figurations of spirits and mediums (Lambek 2002, 2016), dreams and artifacts (Stewart 2017). These emphases have been equally accompanied by a recognition of the place of power in the production of the past (Cohen 1994; Trouillot 1995): the uses of history and their contending validities, which include the constitutive politics of historiography as bound to the very nature of the academic-historical archive (Guha 1983, 1997; Klein 1999; Chakrabarty 2000, 2015; Pandey 2001; Thapar 2002, 2005; Schmitt 2012; Amin 2016; see also Malkki 1995; Hartman 1997, 2007; Scott 2005; Banerjee, 2006).

Taken together, at least three critical yet convergent emphases have come to the fore. To begin with, diverse admissions that forms of historical consciousness vary in their degree of symbolic elaboration, their ability to pervade multiple contexts, and their capacity to capture people's imaginations, between and across socio-spatial groupings. Moreover, salient suggestions that history does not only refer to events and processes "out there," but that it exists as a negotiated resource at the core of shifting, temporal-spatial configurations of historical worlds and subject formation. Finally, urgent reminders not only of the coupling of modern historiography with national imaginaries but also of the haunting presence of a reified West in widespread beliefs in historical progress (Dube 2017).

It follows that historical representation has been found as being made up of overlaying yet contending protocols of meaning and power, time and space, the oral and the written, the genealogical and the national, and dominance and difference (Herzfeld 1991; Amin 1995; Mayaram 1997; Shyrock 1997; Dube 1998; Price 1998; Skaria 1999; Gold and Gujar 2002; Banerjee-Dube 2007; Chaturvedi 2007; Thurner 2011). Alongside such emphases, bids to articulate the past have combined the desire to prudently probe and narrate social terrains with the impulse to critically articulate and affirm them (Dening 1991, 1996; Cohen 1994; Trouillot 1995; Clendinnen 1999; Redfield 2000; Dube 2004a; Scott 2005; Pandey 2006; Chakrabarty 2015; Amin 2016; see also Nandy 1995). As shall soon be discussed, such dispositions have found discrete configurations in recent scholarship on subjects of "heritage," turning on archeology, ethnography, and history.

Colony and Empire

Based upon the interchanges between anthropology, history, and related critical perspectives, on offer is another set of crucial explorations. My reference is to studies that center on colonial cultures of rule (among others, see Comaroff and Comaroff 1991, 1992, 1997; Thomas 1994, 1997; Pels 1997; Stoler and Cooper 1997; Stoler 2002, 2008). At stake are challenges to overarching representations of colony and empire.[19]

To begin with, exploring the practices, representations, and boundaries of settler peoples, imperial agents, and evangelizing missionaries, such scholarship has not only revealed the crucial dividing lines between different colonial agents and diverse imperial agendas. It has equally underscored that such conflicting interests and contending visions could often drive a single colonial project (Comaroff 1989; Stoler 1989, 2002; Thomas 1994; Sivaramakrishan 1999; Wolfe 1999; Dube 2004a, 2010).

Moreover, there have been close analyses of the relationship between the metropolis and the colony, the mutual shaping of European processes and colonial pasts. Such endeavors have explored the ways in which impulses of empire and their reworking in the colonies brought about changes at the core of Western history (Mignolo 1995; Said 1995; Stoler 1995a; Cohn 1996; Gikandi 1996; Mehta 1999; van der Veer 2001; see also Burton 1998; Chatterjee 2001; Collingham 2011). They have extended to the ways that there were conjunctions and contradictions – speaking of disciplines of modernity, as it were – between bids to "control" subject groups at home and efforts to "civilize" subject populations in the colonies (Davin 1978; Comaroff and Comaroff 1992: 265–295; Keane 2007).

Third, there have been imaginative analyses of colonial processes – as shaping the margins and the metropolises – that turned on: space, time, language, the body, and the law (Fabian 1986; Mitchell 1988; Vaughan 1991; Arnold 1993; Mignolo 1995; Merry 2001; Goswami 2004; Rabasa 2011; see also Hamann 2020); imperial travel, exhibitory orders, museum collections, colonial representations, and material exchanges (Rafael 1988; Thomas 1991; Pratt 1992; Coombes 1994; Scott 1994; Bennett 1995, 2004; Grewal 1996; Wolfe 1999; Fabian 2000; Rabasa 2000; Henare 2009; Mackenzie 2010); "culture," consumption, art, and literature (Tarlo 1996; Pinney 1997, 2004; Guha-Thakurta

2005; Mathur 2007); and gender, sexuality, race, and desire (Gutiérrez 1991; Sinha 1995, 2006; Manderson and Jolly 1997; Mani 1998; Stoler 2002).

Finally, a few more issues warrant attention. We have been reminded the importance of tracking the interplay between historical representation, political economy, and state formation (Cooper 1996; Coronil 1997; Birla 2009; Bhattacharya 2018). Newer nuanced understandings of culture and power have emerged bound to powerful reminders that gender and sexuality sutured and structured formations of empire (e.g., McClintock 1995). And there have been incisive explorations of the colonial experience in the making of the modern world. These involve the linkages between Enlightenment and empire, race and reason, and the past and the present (Berman 2004; Dubois 2004, 2006; Fischer 2004; Baucom 2005; Gregory 2007; Agnani 2013; Simpson 2014; see also Muthu 2003; Scott 2005). They extend to the formidable rethinking of the past and the present of the disciplines in view of their linkages with colony and empire alongside their connections with gender and nation (Chakrabarty 2000; Mohanty 2003).

Nations and Nationalisms

It follows that understandings of the tensions and textures of empire have been accompanied by analyses of the contentions and characteristics of the nation.[20] There have been prescient challenges to pervasive projections of nation, nation-state, and nationalism as expressing primordial patterns and innate designs, which turn upon each other, spatially and temporally. Nations and nationalisms, although among the most consequential institutions and imaginings of recent times, have appeared as social artifacts and historical processes, variously displaying attributes of what Benedict Anderson (1983) famously called "imagined communities."

On the one hand, astute studies of the processual construction of nationalisms have tracked their fabrications and fantasies (Herzfeld 1987; Alonso 1994; van der Veer 1994; Tarlo 1996; Mayaram 1997; Pandey 2001; Ohnuki-Tierney 2002; see also Kelly 1991; Shyrock 1997). These entail not only pedagogy and performance of the nation (Bhabha 1990: 291–322), but also scandals of the state and citizen (Sunder Rajan 2003; Saldaña-Portillo 2016). On the other hand, there has been keen recognition that such patterns and procedures of power, far being simply ideological errors, are formative facts of social worlds. They bear densely, often violently, ontological attributes that are palpably visceral and visual (Alonso 1994; Amin 1995; Malkki 1995;

Herzfeld 1997; Butalia 1998; Kelly and Kaplan 2001; van der Veer 2001; Pinney 2004; Pandey 2006; Jha 2016). Here, the pedagogies, performances, and practices of nation and state inhere in their everyday identifications and quotidian configurations, even as nationalisms and nation-states unravel varieties of disciplinary power, spatial-temporal imaginaries, cultural cartographies, and racial ethnic-cleansing techniques (Herzfeld 1987, 1991; Malkki 1995; Hansen and Stepputat 2001; Ohnuki-Tierney 2002; Tarlo 2003; Rufer 2010; Middleton 2015).

Clearly, the figuration of nationalisms and nations as dominant "projects" does not occlude their formative distinctions. As part of wider fields of counter-colonial politics (Kelly 1991), subaltern endeavors accessed and exceeded, straddled, and subverted the practices and premises of middle-class nationalism, often expressing a supplementary politics of the nation (Dube 2004b: 16–20; consider also Ileto 1979; Dubois 2004). At the same time, middle-class anticolonial nationalisms articulated their own differences by translating and transforming European democratic and republican traditions, Enlightenment and post-Enlightenment principles, in order to sieve the images and ideas of the sovereign nation and the citizen subject through forceful filters of the subjugated homeland and the colonized subject (Chatterjee 1993; see also Dubois 2006). Such difference and distinction further mark the presence of gender and sexuality as shaping elemental aspects of authority and alterity at the heart of nations and nationalisms – in their dominant and subaltern avatars (among many, many others, out of South Asia, consider Menon and Bhasin 1998; Sarkar 2001; Roy 2005; Sinha 2006). And so, too, reaching beyond the selfsame, spatial-temporal identifications of the nation-state as settled verities – while thinking through "methodological nationalism" – alterities and identities of state and nation appear as bearing intimacies and contentions with transnational imperatives and global transactions (Axel 2001; Goswami 2004).

Makeovers of Modernity

It should be evident that new emphases in historical and anthropological enquiries have implicitly and explicitly emphasized the requirements of rethinking modernity and the modern, their processes and persuasions. In place of exclusive images, analytical abstractions, and formalist frames that attend these notions, the divergent articulations of modernity and contending expressions of the modern have emerged as attributes of crisscrossing yet particular histories and cultures, identities and differences, and times and spaces (Gilroy 1993; Comaroff and Comaroff 1997, 2009; Coronil 1997; Poole 1997; Donham 1999; Redfield 2000; van der Veer 2001; Voekel 2002; Meyer and Pels 2003; Dube 2004a, 2011; Dubois 2004, 2006; Rappaport 2005; Bear 2007; Pandian 2009; Trouillot 2010; see also Taussig 1997, 2004; Mbembe 2001; Scott 2005; Saler 2012). At the same time, exactly such diversity, its vernacular and plural character, arrive as already influenced by likenesses of an imaginary yet tangible Western modernity (Coronil 1996, 1997; Ferguson 1999; Chakrabarty 2000, 2002; Mitchell 2000; Harootunian 2002; Saldaña-Portillo 2003; Fischer 2004; Overmeyer-Velázquez 2006; Weidman 2006; Seth 2007; Dube 2009, 2019; Rao 2009; Dube and Banerjee-Dube 2019). Rather than invocations of "alternative" or "early" or "multiple" modernities (e.g., Daedalus 1998, 2000), at stake are explorations of modernity and its subjects – human and nonhuman – as simultaneously shaping and shaped by contradictory and contended processes of meaning and power. To be thought through are hetero-temporal-spatial procedures that are incessantly articulated but also out-of-joint with themselves (Dube 2017a and 2017b; see also Banerjee 2020).

Coda: Closing Queries

In the twenty-first century, salient strands of sociocultural anthropology appear to have gradually, principally pulled away from histories and archives, often avowing instead ethics, philosophy, and immediacies of dissonance and dominance. At the same time, critical histories and imaginative ethnographies are meaningfully articulating cultures, politics, and economies in the common production of the present and the past. Against the grain of the methodological disavowal of history and along the grain of its expressive articulations, a few distinct tendencies warrant mention. Each of these inclinations straddles questions of subalterns and margins, histories and pasts, colony and empire, nations and nationalisms, and state and modernity.

The first of these trends involves the critical study of "heritage" – including its emergence, sponsored by UNESCO, in the last part of the twentieth century – understood as at once "a hegemonic, highly institutionalized project of commemoration that is productive of collective identities ... *and* the counter-memories it oppresses" and engenders (De Cesari 2010: 625, emphasis added). On the one hand, at stake is the existence of compound heritage discourses-practices that reveal "the past [as] contested, conflictual, and multiply constituted" (Meskell 2012: 1). To be found here also are endeavors that variously query the liberal ethos of inheritance as well as objectifications of the modern state, registering thereby "the cracks, contingencies, and omissions of contemporary heritage regimes" (Geismar 2015: 80). On the other hand, we are in the face as well of the commitments of international, national, and "local" heritage regimes themselves to rather more circumscribed, singular notions of the past, often turning on the concept-entity of the nation-state. These are frequently accompanied by bids to suppress multiple constituencies or narratives that draw together "negative," "absent," and "difficult" heritage (Meskell 2002; Macdonald 2009) as well as "counter-heritage" (Byrne 2014) and "subversive archaisms" (Herzfeld 2019). Such deep entanglements register the productions of pasts by state and subaltern as well as by NGO, neoliberal, and supranational governance. Unsurprisingly, all of this occurs amidst the uneasy interplay and varied contentions of expressions of empire and imperatives of nation alongside claims of cosmopolitanism and demands of nationalism. Foregrounded forthwith are confounded, even combustible, labours of archeology and anthropology, enacted under contemporary regimes of heritage and history (Olwig 1999; Meskell 2009, 2018; Winter 2014; Geismar 2015; Herzfeld 2016; Kaltmeier and Rufer 2017).

A second tendency centers on a shift announcing that earlier historical anthropologies and cultural histories of Christianity (Comaroff and Comaroff 1986, 1991, 1997; Hefner 1993; Scott 1994; Landau 1995; Peel 1995; Austin-Broos 1997; Larson 1997; Makdisi 1997, 2008; Meyer 1999; Peterson 1999; see also Mignolo 1995), their colonial aspects and vernacular attributes, can be revisited in salient ways. They can be read and rendered, imaginatively and critically, in terms of an anthropology of Christianity, indeed of anthropologies of the secular, including especially those of an archival imagination (Robbins 2004; Cannell 2006, 2010; Engelke 2007; Keane 2007; Mosse 2012; Curley 2018; see also Asad 1993, 2003).

The final set of inclinations consists of studies that have variously explored formations of slavery as well as those of settler-colonialisms in the production of modern worlds. Such critical discussions bear very wide implications. Here, race and slavery – alongside "reason" and "freedom" – emerge as lying at the core of colony and nation, mercantilism and modernity, and industrialism and the Enlightenment, as defining their mutual makeovers and crossovers, their constitutive tensions and contentions (Dubois 2004, 2006; Scott 2005; Blackburn 2011; Beckert 2014; Guasco 2014; Betancor 2017; Gerbener 2018). At the same time, it is crucial to read such scholarship together with astute understandings of "indigeneity" and "sovereignty" as well as the politics of "recognition" and "refusal" in the articulations of settler-colonialisms being constitutive of modernity and nation, race and state (for instance, Wolfe 1999; Povinelli 2002, 2016; Barker 2011; Simpson 2014; Bhandar 2018; see also, Goeman 2013; King 2019).

And so, at the end, we return to where we started. On the one hand, the dichotomy between the savage and the civilized that defined the beginnings of history and anthropology as institutionalized enquiries has been left behind by salient strands of critical knowledge. On the other hand, in newer and older avatars, the antinomy and its implications, especially unraveled as hierarchies of otherness, continue to haunt, surreptitiously and frontally, our worlds at large. None of this requires emphasis in the ruins we inhabit. Yet a question still hangs, a restless specter as it were. How are we to read and render the human sciences as disciplines of modernity ahead of always prior images of the native and already *a priori* imaginaries of the modern (Dube et al. nd)? The images and imaginaries occupy epistemic mirrors that abound, scattered as shards everywhere we see and seek, look and find.

Notes

1 A few clarifications are in order at the outset. In speaking of anthropology, my reference is to the sociocultural branch of the discipline, which draws in of course ethnography and ethnology. This means further that I do not attend to issues of archeology, despite their connections with questions explored in the chapter, whether in the work of, say, a scholar such as Moses Finley or in the articulations, explored ahead, of critical heritage studies. Alongside, I bracket specific considerations also of twentieth-century philosophers of history, from R. G. Collingwood through to Hayden White, including the influence of the former on "interpretivist" anthropology, especially via the work of E. E. Evans-Pritchard, and of the latter on strands of history and ethnography. On another note, it might be argued that lineaments of scholarship in vast polities such as China and Russia were intrinsically different from the intellectual formations that this chapter discusses: but it is my submission that the institutionalization of history, ethnology/anthropology, and folklore as modern enquiries in these distinct empires and nations might be better understood as emerging from conversations and contentions with salient tendencies elsewhere. Furthermore, the chapter cites almost exclusively works and translations in the English language: on the interplay of anthropology and history, references to scholarship in French are to be found in Naepels (2010) and Viazzo (2003), the latter discussing also works in other European languages. Finally, concerning the questions addressed here, including the references that shore up the discussion, my bid is toward a critically indicative, inclusive endeavor – instead of a more narrowly exclusive, exhaustive exercise.

2 Here are to be found discussions that project a step-by-step opening of social-cultural history toward anthropology and that further portray

exceptional anthropological ancestors as heeding the call of the past till
the two disciplines inevitably, inexorably embrace each other, from the
1970s onward. While present in publications, such dispositions are even
more dispersed in the classroom and the seminar, pedagogies cast in terms
of "schools," "masters," and their "greatest hits," with especial importance accorded to programmatic statements and ensuing debates (Evans-
Pritchard 1961; Schapera 1962; Thomas 1963; Thompson 1972, 1977; Cohn
1980, 1981). At stake are assumptions, exactly uncovered by Brian Axel
(2002b, 13), concerning history and anthropology as "whole and complete
in themselves," as principally awaiting a "dialogue" between their already
given methodologies. Against the grain of such orientations, this chapter
attempts to think through and open up the terms, textures, and transformations of anthropology and history – their common grounds, constitutive conceits, formative presumptions, disciplinary dissensions, mutual
makeovers, and substantive contributions – including in conversation
with other studies of the interplay between these disciplines (e.g., Kelly
and Kaplan 1990; Krech 1991; Hastrup 1992; Faubion 1993; Pels 1997;
Reddy 1999; Axel 2002a; Viazzo 2003; "Anthropology and Time," *Annales*
2010; Naepels 2010; Murphy et al. 2011; Palmié and Stewart 2016; Pooley
2018; Palmié and Stewart 2019; Coello de la Rosa and Mateo Dieste 2020.
Dube [2007b] considers the interplay between anthropology and history in
South Asia as part of a larger story).

3 While the constitutive attributes of the dichotomy have been often registered for the anthropological discipline (e.g., Stocking 1987, 1992, 1995;
Trouillot 1991), I am extending the reach of the argument to modern,
institutionalized, disciplinary history, which shall be clarified soon. It
bears emphasis that, even more than the other parts of the chapter, this
section is based on wide reading but cites only those indicative references
that would be useful to readers.

4 This is not to deny prior formations of the modernity of the Renaissance
and of the empires of southern Europe in the New World (Mignolo 1995;
Dube and Banerjee-Dube 2019). But a discussion of their presence in
anthropology and history as modern enquiries is outside the scope of this
chapter.

5 Stocking's (1987) astute account of the crystallization of "civilization" and
"culture" in Western Europe across the first half of the nineteenth century
is monumental, synthetic scholarship (see also Stocking 1992, 1995.)

6 While this chapter cannot do justice to this issue, I will throughout attempt
to point toward such surpluses of significance and their escape from prior
schemas and *a priori* readings.

7 Let me confess to not being able to consider here questions such as those
of the persistence of "polygenism" and of "degenerationism," especially as
bound to biblical anthropology.

8 Considering such questions, it is important to keep in mind the larger
reshaping of Boasian anthropology as well as the widening breach between
British and US anthropology, such that while both emphasized synchrony
they bore different evaluations of culture (Stocking 1992: 118–150, 353–357;
1995: 233–441; Dube 2007a: 52–53, n. 33, 36).

9 I need to acknowledge here my profound debt to critical writings on
indigeneity and sovereignty – in this case especially the work of Audra

Simpson (e.g. 2020) – for impelling me to rethink the genealogies of disciplines and the unsaid of their chroniclers. I propose to undertake such re-readings in Dube et al. (nd).

10 This discussion of the institutionalization of historiography and historicism brings together a score and more writings. Here let me only orient the reader to works by Iggers (1995, 2012), Kelley (1998: 244–272), Stocking (1987: 20–25), and Zammito (2002).

11 Returning to pathways that have been opened up yet mainly forgotten within disciplinary practice, it is worth contrasting the historicist tradition under discussion with the historical narratives of the nineteenth-century French scholar Jules Michelet. Here, Michelet's actual procedures of research and writing can be read as recasting "hermeneutic" and "scientific" methods in order to foreground the salient but repressed "subject of history." This also intimated the requirements of historical writing to live up to its threefold contract – "scientific, political, and literary"– with modern political democratic constituencies (Rancière 1994, 2004).

12 Social-scientific history of this kind, focusing on economy and society and concerned with structures and dynamics of the past, often of the long run, gradually became salient to the profession for most of the twentieth century. In this chapter, I do not account for the varied articulations and distinct tendencies of such historiography: in its search for underlying patterns and processes these tendencies could principally bracket the meanings and actions of historical subjects, which I see as crucial to the intersections and remaking of anthropology and history.

13 Interestingly, in their self-presentation the Annales went onto emphasize the rupture with *événementielle* history-writing, variously foregrounding the nation, of Charles-Victor Langlois and Charles Seignobos rather than the influence of Durkheim. (I thank Mario Rufer for this point.) My sense is that this has to do with the increasing emphasis of "autonomy" of disciplines from the 1910s through to the 1960s. The issue needs further exploration.

14 On the one hand should we not ask if the formative "structural histories" crafted by the Annales school deprived Western "history of its human subject, its links to a generally political and specifically democratic agenda, and its characteristic mode of representing its subject's manner of being in the world, namely, narrative" (White 1994, xi)? On the other hand did not Fernand Braudel's influential writings render vast parts of the Mediterranean world as islands floating outside the currents of civilization and history, further casting as ahistorical the sphere of everyday material culture as compared to the historical dynamism of early modern mercantilism (Braudel 1973; Medick 1995: 42–44)?

15 Issues of "autonomy" in academic enquiry assumed immense importance from the 1910s through to at least the 1960s (and after). They are to be discussed in Dube et al. nd.

16 Concerning these three tendencies, only the later writings of Mintz (1985) and Wolf (1982) – alongside those of Roseberry (1989) – generally find mention in discussions of anthropology and history.

17 In this context, it is crucial to consider also traditions of scholarship as represented by "oral history" (Vansina 1985) as well as the ethnographic

history of the "Melbourne School" (Clendinnen 1987, 1999; Dening 1991, 1995, 1996).

18 The way much of this came together in the last quarter of the twentieth century becomes clear from the following: the urgent political-theoretical intervention of Said (1978; see also Grosrichard 1998) not only had a ripple effect on postcolonial perspectives as unraveling the presence of the colony in the making of modernity and on subaltern studies as interrogating the modern nation-state, but came to define critical sensibilities that variously articulated the scholarship on the cusp of history and anthropology discussed ahead.

19 It bears mention that the emphases of these writings have not necessarily been in accord with dominant tendencies within subaltern studies and postcolonial perspectives, which can project colonial power as a dystopian totality (Guha 1997; see also Guha 2004) or/and trace a formative ambivalence as fracturing and splitting colonial cultural discourse (Bhabha 1994). Moreover, authoritative formations of decolonial understandings have little patience for such "revisionist" understandings of colonialism. Finally, at the same time, the wider interest in questions of colonial representations and writings was equally evident in tendencies such as "new historicism" (Greenblatt 1991).

20 Such scholarship on the nation from the 1980s onwards rested upon key conjunctions between historical anthropologies, subaltern studies, critical histories, postcolonial perspectives, and influential writings such as those by Anderson (1983) and Corrigan and Sayer (1985).

3 Figures of Dissonance
Dalit Religions and Anthropological Archives[1]

This chapter revisits earlier ethnographic writing and anthropological assumption – as well as draws upon more recent historical scholarship – in order to reconsider thorny questions of Dalit "religions."[2] In doing so it stays with the salience of using prior ethnographies and the issues they have raised as an archive, while underscoring questions regarding the terms of identities and politics in our present. As we shall see, all of this puts a distinct spin on the explorations in this book of the disciplines of modernity now as underpinned by the contending pathways and crisscrossing byways of the "native" and the "modern," which underlie the anthropological archives discussed ahead.

It should barely be surprising that, as category and process, religion does not appear in these pages as a bounded and *a priori* realm – an innate and static repository – of the sacral and the metaphysical (Asad 1993; McCutheon 1997). It is understood instead as entailing experiential and historical meanings and motivations, perception and practices, and symbols and rituals, which are intimately bound to formations of power and its negotiations. Defined by such processual-meaningful, substantive-symbolic, and dominant-dissonant attributes, religions lie at the core of social worlds and their transformations, simultaneously shaped by as well shaping these historical terrains (Kelly and Kaplan 1990; Dube 1998: 4–7; Banerjee-Dube and Dube 2009: 5–7). Alongside, the chapter – in tune with this book – approaches archives as ongoing, unfinished, open-ended procedures; articulates identities as contradictory and contingent processes of meaning and power, which inhabit the core of modernity; and understands politics as intimating relations of authority and alterity, dispersed yet intimate, which access and exceed governmental commands and conceits in their own ways (Dube 2004, 2017).

It is by combining such emphases that I seek to unravel critical attributes of Dalit religions and their distinct formations. Here, I explore

DOI: 10.4324/9781003347569-3

especially the following issues: the nature of power in the caste order when viewed both from Dalit perspectives and from the Dalit position; the historical (political-economic *and* cultural-discursive) construction of caste under colonial dominance and imperial rule; the terms not only of the Dalit's absolute exclusion from but their unequal inclusion in the social order; Dalit responses to hierarchy and authority, which look further than their endeavors exclusively within institutionalized power relations turning on state and governance; and, finally, the intimate intermeshing of religion and politics, each broadly understood.[3]

Overture

It warrants emphasis that the last two decades or so have seen a forceful ferment in Dalit as well as Bahujan worlds. Such ferment and these force-fields have extended across academic and activist arenas, intellectual and political terrains.[4] Here, committed Dalit and Bahujan protagonists have been joined by other, concerned academics and activists in public and scholarly domains – in an increasingly intolerant India (and in a world more and more commandeered by the entitled and the tyrannical, at large). What I wish to emphasize is that two contrasting considerations, overlapping imperatives, stand out in the present conjuncture.

On the one hand, a constitutive heterogeneity characterizes such fields, these force-fields, of scholarship and politics. Without drawing an extensive inventory, consider the formative differences – in thought and practice – between the political outlook of Chandrabhan Prasad (2006) and Jignesh Mevani (2022); between the epistemic concerns of Gopal Guru (2009) and Sukhdeo Thorat (2009); between the analytical frames of G. Aloysius (1997) and Kancha Ilaih (1996); between the interpretive emphases of Charu Gupta (2016) and Anupama Rao (2009); between the critical outlook of Sanal Mohan (2015) and Suryakant Waghmore (2013); between the engaging immediacies of Anand Teltumbde (2017, see also 2018) and Suraj Yengde (2019); and between the testimonial textures of Bama (2008) and Sharmila Rege (2006). This is not only *how it is* but *how it has to be*.[5] Such is the case since, on the other hand, not only the protagonists that I have named but all those involved in Dalit-Bahujan formations and their study are passionately convinced of their own persuasions and positions. All this follows from the necessarily contentious nature of Dalit-Bahujan fields as well as the formatively contending character of intellectual terrains studying these domains.[6]

The point now is that I do not wish to readily legislate upon these differences. Rather, I submit that such distinctions are themselves indicative at once of the enormous heterogeneity as well as the necessarily contending attributes of Dalit-Bahujan domains, exactly as part of our conflict-ridden worlds. And there is much to be learned from such contrariness. None of this is to deny my own preferences in scholarship as in politics: but I also refuse to simply, scholastically champion and institute these preferences, since what I do not like will not disappear as though it were a mere analytical nightmare. Put differently, in keeping with the tenor of this book, I eschew avowing an adversarial approach that analytically privileges its own arguments concerning what the world "is" and its understanding "ought" to be, in order to, quickly disavow uncomfortable, contending claims that yet inhabit social terrains. This issue will soon become clearer. The point now is that it is while recognizing the critical contention and the formative ferment centering on Dalit-Bahujan formations as *constitutive* of our worlds that I proffer, in a spirit of dialogue, my thoughts and provocations. These rest upon particular registers of historical anthropology, critical ethnography, and their interplay.

It bears mention that my own work on Dalit subjects over the past three decades has followed distinct yet overlapping trajectories: a history of the Satnami caste-sect of Chhattisgarh over the last 200 years (Dube 1992: 121–156, 1998); the place of Dalits within evangelical entanglements (Dube 1995, 1998, 2004a, 2010); Dalit articulations of the law and the state, legalities, and illegalities (Dube 1993; 1996a, 1996b, 1998, 2004a); and an ongoing exploration of the art of (and my friendship with) the expressionist artist Savi Sawarkar (Dube 2012: 251–267; 2013b). Put differently, my focus has been principally on Dalit histories, religions, and their processes as not simply confined to the institutionalized political relations centering on the state and its subjects. That is, rather than the politics of the state being the principal optic of understanding, I approach politics and states through processes of society and culture, including the routine interchanges between all these arenas. The corollary to such an orientation is the fact that I understand power and politics not simply in terms of institutionalized relations of state and nation, but as entailing rather more diffuse, even intimate, matrices and relationships of authority, as was insinuated earlier. At stake are procedures of labor and caste, ritual and myth, gender and sexuality, and affect and embodiment.

All of this has critical connotations for just what it is that I mean by Dalit religions, including their enmeshments with authority and alterity. Now, Dalit religions spell for me historical processes of meaning and power, labor and gender, ritual and practice that centrally turn on caste, its containments and contestations. Here are to be found ideas and actions that heterogeneously yet simultaneously entail the social and the symbolic, the bodily and the mythic, the immanent and the sacral, the experiential and the emotional, and the sexual and the spiritual.[7] At the same time, these ensembles appear ever enmeshed with formations of caste, which include at once dominant conventions based on ritual authority *and* popular precepts with contending dispositions to hierarchy, impurity, and worship, a question that shall be clarified soon. My point is that the nature of caste and its modalities of power can be unraveled only by admitting that Dalit presence, position, and perspectives have haunted and shaped these procedures.[8]

Consider now formidable voices challenging Dalit-Bahujan subjugation: from saint poets such as Chokha Mela and Sant Nirmala, Basavanna and Sorayabai; to key figures including Ravidas and Ghasidas, Mahima Swami and Parsuram that founded popular-religious formations of sect and caste; and onto modern intellectuals and activists such as Phule and Mangoo Ram, Periyar and Ambedkar. On the one hand, in different ways all these critics acutely registered the configurations of authoritative religion and their persuasions – especially, the *doxa* and *orthopraxis* of Hinduism – as constitutive of domination and subordination within matrices of caste. On the other hand, their critiques variously rearranged the incessant interplay between ritual and power in distinct formulations of religion and politics, imbuing these with novel meanings. Taken together, learning from these entwined protocols, my bid is to allow Dalit religions to possibly hold up a mirror to attributes of authority and alterity at the core of the caste order across different faiths in South Asia.[9]

To be sure, no term is perfect. In the manner that I have used it, my preference for Dalit religions – over, say, Dalit "cultures" or Dalit "identities" – centers on the manner in which this term does not shy away from but lays bare the overlaying schemes of social subjection that articulate caste and its constituents. Here are to be found adroit alchemies of ritual authority, historical practice, colonial transformations, and modern makeovers that have shaped the subordination and subversion, meanings and actions of Dalit communities. Once more, these designs of dominance and dissonance, palpable and spectral, have been woven into, and help unravel, the fabrics of caste and power at large.

This registered, I would like to make two clarifications. First, I return in this paper to intellectual-political issues that are often approached as matters that are already settled, even resolutely resolved.[10] My going back to such questions is a bid to ask: Can we speak differently today about earlier scholarship, using it as an archive, seeking not dismissal or novelty or both – but rather a re-visitation of queries that continue to haunt and that we exorcise at some peril? What might we gain by abjuring a readily analytical, sharply scholastic stance, in order instead to approach these archives by reading them against as well as along the grain of their exclusive assumption? Can this make possible the learning of critical verities from these now reconfigured archives? Second, to speak of *Dalit* as at once a category and a mode of a people's self-description that challenges their subordination has key consequences.[11] At stake are acute issues of the politics of naming, urgent demands on tasks of understanding. Revealed once more are the inadequacies of ready separations between religious-ritual patterns and social-political processes, in this case considering discussions of Dalit formations.

Archiving Anthropology

Dalit religions have ever turned on charged questions. As already mentioned, I return in this chapter to aspects of anthropological scholarship of the past and the issues it raised, using it as an archive of the present. Does the alleged extreme impurity and the ritual-practices of Dalits place them outside the caste order? Do they have their entirely separate religions? Or, does the very ritual lowness of the Dalits hierarchically yet vitally link them to other castes? Does this linkage to other castes exclusively entail an encompassing, consensual caste ideology of purity and pollution? Is Dalit religion, then, primarily a lower form of that of those higher up in the caste order, as Louis Dumont and Michael Moffatt once argued? (Dumont 1970; Moffatt 1979; Deliège 1992). Indeed, the debate that is reflected by these queries was well summarized by Moffatt (1979) almost four decades ago. Yet, the questions continue, whether in sanctioned or disavowed states.

When scholars such as Dumont and Moffatt present Dalits as primarily reproducing the ritual hierarchy of purity and pollution, itself projected as a homogeneous scheme, their emphases are beset by at least three critical problems. First, by focusing singularly on purity/pollution as cementing a principally normative caste structure they externalize the terms and textures of power that inhere in caste formations, especially the modalities of domination and subordination in the caste order. Second, they underplay the other key matrices that shape caste. I have in mind configurations of ritual kingship/dominance, colonial governance, non-Brahman religions, postcolonial politics, and the modern state as constitutive of caste. Third and finally, such emphases underplay the creations within Dalit religions of novel meanings and distinctive practices.

And what of the various scholarly and commonplace positions that stress the radical disjunction of Dalit norms and practices from the caste order?[12] Often well-meaning, such proposals bear their own difficulties. First, while these projections understand the manner in which the ideologies and relationships of caste *unequally exclude* Dalit peoples from several processes, they tend to overlook how caste arrangements also *hierarchically include* Dalit castes in other arrangements. Moreover, the arguments often underplay the expressions of hierarchy and authority in the religions of Dalits themselves. Here are to be found ritual articulations that involve practices of endogamy, occupation, commensality, and interactions with other Dalit castes. Finally, the emphases on the innate "autonomy" of Dalit religions usually overlook the matrices and meanings, processes and practices that structure and suture caste.

Taken together, under issue is the key question of power: specifically, the presence of power at the core of caste; this is to say, the wider interplay between meaning and power, religion and authority in caste society in South Asia. And as a corollary to this, a related issue concerns the ways in which the caste order is imagined irrevocably in the mirrors of Hindu society. That is, among other processes, colonial cultures, South Asian Islam, and Indian Christianity are understood as impinging only externally, derivatively in the shaping and reshaping of configurations of caste, hierarchy, and power, which remain innately, originally Hindu.

First things first. Consider Louis Dumont's exclusive preoccupation with a normative order presided over by the Brahman and defined by logics-techniques of purity and pollution. Now, the writings of Dumont – and his supporters – broadly encompass *artha* (economic and political power) within *dharma* (ideology and status). Here, the ritual hierarchy of purity and pollution fixes the extreme poles of the ranking of castes, while leaving "power" only a residual role in affecting this ordering in the middle. At the same time, it is equally important that "materialist" critiques of Dumont have tended to replicate his absolute separation of and opposition between ideology and power. Here, such critics have tended to emphasize that caste is "essentially" a matter of economic and political power. Thus, ideology – or, the ritual hierarchy of purity and pollution – is only a gloss to basic inequities and social divisions.[13] Unsurprisingly, both sides – that is, Dumont and his materialist critics – ignore the way *power is structured into the cultural schemes, the pervasive meanings, of purity and pollution.* In a word, exactly these elisions allow us to underscore that power is central to the normative, meaningful order of purity-pollution.

There is more to the picture. I refer to the work of Nicholas Dirks (1987), Gloria Raheja (1988), and Declan Quigley (1993) that has focused – in different ways – on the ideological, religious, and cultural character of kingship and the dominant-caste. Actually, this debate once more returns us to the issue of power in the caste order. We just noted that the influential arguments of Dumont encompass power within the ritual hierarchy of purity and pollution, and thus render it epiphenomenal. In contrast, the writings of Dirks (1987), Raheja (1988), and Quigley (1993) open up possibilities for discussions of the intermeshing of caste structure, ritual form, and cultural attributes of dominance. At the same time, they also tend to locate power, almost exclusively, in constructs of ritually and culturally constituted kingship and dominant-caste. The different sides and sites of these ethnographic archives uncertainly invoke and articulate the Ur-distinction between the "native" and the "modern" at the core of anthropology and history as disciplines of modernity, an issue to which I shall return.

The point now is that these distinct positions – an exclusive emphasis on the hierarchical concerns of purity and pollution, which brackets/ removes power from religion; and the somewhat singular embeddings of caste and power within a culturally central, ritually fashioned kingship and dominant-caste – as opposed propositions appear as mirror images. On the one hand, the perspective of the Brahman, at the hands of Dumont (1970), Moffatt (1979), and their companions; on the other hand, the outlook of the little-king or the dominant-caste at the behest of Dirks (1987), Quigley (1993), Raheja (1988), and the like-minded.

Interregnum One: Dalit Interruptus

Whatever happened to the Dalits? Actually, approaching these issues from the position and perspective of Dalits throws a different light on the nature of power in caste society in South Asia. Consider the low ritual status of these groups and their exclusion from the web of relationships defined by service castes, especially the barber (*nai*), the washer-man (*dhobi*), and the grazier in everyday life. All of this underscores that the normative hierarchy of purity and pollution and the principles of a ritually central kingship/dominant-caste should not be seen as separate and opposed principles. Rather, they constitute intertwined cultural schemes, both grounded in relationships of power within the caste order. These distinct but overlapping schemes of ritual power have worked together and reinforced each other in the subordination and definition of Dalit communities. And this has happened entirely in conjunction with colonial transformations of caste, especially across the nineteenth century. Here, the anthropological archives explored above envision caste as principally Indian, even inherently Hindu, and approach its colonial transformations as essentially external to these formations, influencing caste from the outside rather than reconstituting its orders from within.[14]

Transformations of Caste

Historical shifts and mutations during the colonial period led to a wider restructuring of caste and power, as profoundly bound to the normative hierarchy of purity/pollution *and* the ritual centrality of kingship/dominant-caste. The issue warrants discussion. Routinely, questions of the colonial transformations of caste, power, and Dalit identities are approached through a primary focus on the imperial state's impact from the 1860s to 1940s on caste categories and religious communities in census enumeration and representative politics.[15] Such focus on the impact of colonial policies is often accompanied by the highlighting of diverse indigenous non-Brahman movements in western and southern India and increased Christian missionary activity that challenged upper-caste authority. Together, it is argued, the result was the articulation of caste "movements" and Dalit identities, often in the domain of institutionalized politics defined by imperial administration.[16]

Much of this happened, no doubt, yet not quite in the singular ways that are usually insinuated. Indeed, the point is that such exclusive demarcations of imperial transformations overlook other, important makeovers of caste in the colonial period. My reference is to profound changes in political-economy, alongside the intricate meeting, mating, and makeovers of Brahmanical, kingly, and colonial axes of authority. All of this together reshaped caste and power under colony and empire. Needless to say, these developments carry profound import for apprehensions of Dalit religions and histories.[17]

Consider that the exact locations of caste, rural and urban, were constitutively formed and acutely transformed in the nineteenth century. Here, I am speaking not only of discursive-cultural shifts but crucially also of political-economic mutations, making a case for the ways these domains overlap. Thus, we often forget that the Indian village as the locus of caste – in the way these matrices are known to us – emerged principally in the course of the first half of the nineteenth century. This *emergence of the village as the locus of caste in the first half of the nineteenth century* was the outcome of distinct yet overlapping processes, of contentious, contradictory meanings and practices. I cannot recount the convoluted story here, which is drawn from a range of historical scholarship.[18] But allow me to rapidly, telegraphically signal certain major mileposts.

We are in the face of the East India Company's practices of settling borders, of controlling populations, and of maximizing revenues alongside its policies of outright warfare and of quotidian conquest. These led to the redrawing of commons, the reworking of scrubs, the rearranging of forests, alterations in climate, and an emphasis on "settled" socio-spatial subjects and terrains. All of this underlay the emergence of an agrarian order clearly characterized by discrete agricultural castes and petty commodity production, ironing out ambiguities and categorically demarcating distinctions between the "civilized" and the "wild," "field" and "forest," *vana* and *kshetra*. Here is the emergence actually of the exact arenas in which caste as we know it came to be enacted.

Now, these principally settled ethno-scapes and landscapes from the nineteenth century onwards were very different from the formatively shifting terrains that had existed up to the eighteenth century in South Asia. The latter bid us to retrace our steps. For these prior worlds were marked by irregular boundaries between *vana, gochar and kshetra,* forests, commons (as well as shrubs), and fields. Here, nomadic peoples with enormous herds of cattle routinely moved between mountains and plains. Here, shifting cultivators now took up settled agriculture and could again move back to mobile practices all within five generations. Here, ascetics were warriors and traders. Here, *banjaras* and *bagis* were *bahurupiya*s, too. Here, labor and not land was clearly the scarce resource, allowing landless laborers, *adhias* and *kamias* (sharecroppers), to move on in the face of extreme adversity. (Or, to play with Hollywood, when the going got tough, the deprived got going.) The point is that in these critically shifting worlds caste formations and Dalit identities existed, but they did so in a manner quite unfamiliar, even strange, to us. In such terrains, caste relations and Dalit identities were made and unmade, done and undone in ways very different from what came to be in the coming epoch, beginning in the long nineteenth century.[19]

None of this is to readily castigate an all-conquering, ever efficacious, essentially destructive colonialism. Rather, at play in these processes were the coalescing of colonial rule, indigenous authority, and everyday arrangements. Indeed, it was in these emergent spaces of village society that caste formations came to be crystallized, reordering the terms of purity-pollution and ritual kingship – as well as the auspicious-inauspicious – and carrying crucial connotations for Dalit subjects.

Now, as imperial rule, village society, caste arrangements, and Dalit formations were instituted and elaborated in the nineteenth and twentieth centuries, crucial attributes of the colonial order often emerged at the core of caste. Where am I going with this proposition? Following anthropological assumption, sociological scholarship, historical presumption, and quotidian commonsense the caste order is meant to be innately, exclusively, internally Indian. This is to say, caste is irrevocably *desi* (native), seen also often in the image of the Hindu cosmos. And so, following pervasive presuppositions, the colonial presence necessarily remains exterior to the caste order, except by allowing marginal, subaltern, and Dalit groups to challenge and even step outside these schemes.[20]

My point is different, moving in a distinct direction from the innate opposition between colonialism as a foreign implant and caste as an indigenous institution. In a word, I am proposing that the idioms and practices, meanings and signs at the core of colonial cultures – involving the joint energies of the colonizer and colonizer – were often critical in structuring caste and power in their everyday avatars in South Asia. Here are to be found diffuse yet intimate processes elaborating rearranged hierarchies of authority and changed rituals of dominance. Such processes, hierarchies, and rituals drew upon aspects of colonial governance in the constitution of caste and power.

My own work on the Satnami caste-sect in the Chhattisgarh region has played a key role in distilling these emphases. Thus, Satnami oral narratives about village life in the colonial period elaborate the construal of authority within caste society, ordered by the metaphor of *gaonthia zamana* (the era of landlords). This construction-production of authority involved an interleaving of overlapping attributes of dominance. At stake was an intermeshing of the ritual hierarchy of purity and pollution and ritually fashioned kingship with the forms of power derived from the colonial order (Dube 1998).

Such focus on the quotidian symbols, metaphors, and practices of colonial rule as reinforcing other axes of dominance and ritual schemes in order to mutually constitute caste and power has wide implications. It suggests the following four propositions. First, the sway of the state and the enticements of governance are not separate from, outside of, the imaginaries and articulations of caste. Rather, they are internal to, intimate with, and constitutive of this creature and concept, institution and imagining, practice and process. Second, this is true not only of colonial cultures but of postcolonial politics, such that seductions of the state and enchantments of the nation have acquired newer meanings, distinct configurations, and mutating cadences in articulations of caste in independent India. Third and finally, such genealogies and mutations carry critical implications for urban alterations of caste and Dalit formations of politics. Finally, concerning ethnographic archives and Dalit religions, do we not need to critically stay with and carefully think through the uncertain haunting of these terrains by the specters of the "native" and the figures of the "modern" that underlie anthropology, history, and other enquiries as disciplines of modernity? While the first proposition and final query shore up this chapter, the latter two entail issues that I cannot elaborate here.[21]

Interregnum Two: Dalit Expressions

All of this is to say that questions of Dalit religions militate against singular solutions, ready resolutions, intellectual-academic aggrandizements – *a priori* or otherwise, theoretical or empirical, conceptual or factual. Shaped as part of wider hierarchies and relationships of caste, which differ from one region to another, these religions show marked socio-spatial variations. However, even within a particular region, Dalit religions can find distinct expressions in different localities depending on the distribution of landownership and arrangements of authority among castes, which diverge across villages. Further, as was indicated above, Dalit religions have undergone profound changes through state formation, agrarian/urban alterations, and political transformations. The salience of these religions is found precisely within variety, change, and crucial contention. This is an issue that is not only empirical but constitutively critical.[22]

Exclusion and Inclusion

We know of the severe restrictions that have been placed on Dalits.[23] They have been denied entry into Hindu temples and the services of the Brahman *purohit* (priest), spatially segregated unto living quarters at the margins of rural and urban settlements, and excluded from the several sets of ranked relationships, ritual exchanges, and social interactions among discrete castes at the core of quotidian life. Highly-coded prescriptions have governed the appropriate conduct of Dalits in public spaces, including deferential usages of bodily movements and speech patterns before upper-castes; and they have frequently been forbidden the use of markers of honor and status, often signifying kingly status, from modes of transport such as elephants, horses, and palanquins to apparel and accessories such as upper-body garments, turbans, and shoes.[24]

At the same time, the very locations of Dalits in normative hierarchies and centers have included them in the practices and processes of caste. They have exclusively performed the most defiling activities, entailing contact with severely polluting substances, in rural and urban arenas: from the scavenging of waste to work with leather and labor on cremation grounds; and from cleaning toilets and clearing human excrement to rearing so-called unclean animals such as pigs and removing the allegedly impure carcasses of sacred cattle. Some of these tasks constitute the primary occupations of discrete Dalit castes; others they undertake while working as agricultural laborers, poor peasants, and manual laborers.

It bears emphasis that the restrictions imposed upon and defiling tasks undertaken by Dalit castes have simultaneously defined their subordination while placing them at the core of caste. This is because *only they* can perform such pollution-ridden yet essential activities. Unsurprisingly, Dalit presence in the social order has been variously acknowledged, altogether hierarchically and unequally of course: they have received customary dues, especially on ritual occasions, for their caste-sanctioned duties as well as for agricultural labor; their participation has been critical to ceremonies concerning the unity of the village; and their deities – like those of Adivasi groups that bear an ambiguous relationship with the caste order – have been feared for being violent yet venerated as guardians of villages. This is to say that, *in inherently unequal ways*, Dalit religions have been embedded in processes of the Dalits' *exclusion from* as well as *inclusion in* caste hierarchies and ritual processes.

Distinction and Displacement

Dalits have not accepted and experienced such processes simply, passively. Rather, precisely while participating in hierarchical relationships, Dalit actions and understandings have imbued their religions and caste formations with specific distinctions. Here the staggering heterogeneity of Dalit religions has emerged bound to the historical constitution of Hinduism. This historical construction of Hinduism has involved the interplay between Brahmanical hierarchical conventions that emphasize purity-pollution – alongside kingly and dominant-caste centering of ritual kingship – in the partial continuity between humanity and divinity, on the one hand, *and* non-Brahmanical, lower-caste traditions that bear rather different, even contending, orientations to hierarchy and impurity and divinity and worship, on the other (Kapadia 1995; Fuller 2004). Concerning the latter, the links with non-Brahmanical traditions, Dalit religions have displaced, negotiated, and queried normative purity/impurity and ritual hierarchies/centers through ecstatic worship and possession, sensuous devotion and pilgrimage.[25] Sometimes this entails also religious, social, and gendered inversions where men acquire female attributes and Brahmans become impure (Kapadia 1995).

At the same time, it is worth recalling that the origin myths of Dalits all over India have subverted and rejected upper-caste representations of their ritual lowness, yet they have equally frequently done so by retaining notions of their own collective impurity (Moffatt 1979: 120–128; Prakash 2009: 45–55). From the nineteenth century onwards, Dalit communities such as the Satnamis of central India have elaborated new mythic traditions and distinctive caste-sect practices centered on their gurus and a formless god as well as construing novel depictions of deities such as Shiva and Draupadi (Dube 1998). These innovative religious formations question and contest but also rework and reiterate the forms of power encoded in caste schemes of purity-pollution and kingly authority.[26] Still other Dalit groups have participated in spirit cults, propitiating ancestors and ghosts, to articulate as well as reproduce labor bondage and caste hierarchy (Prakash 2009). Dalit membership of sects such as the Kabirpanthis, Dadupanthis, Ravidasis, and Ramnamis has elaborated devotional practices *within* designs of caste distinctions (Lorenzen 1995; see also Hess 2015; Novetzke 2016). Clearly, the common patterns within such variety reside in the fact that Dalit religions have widely expressed the salience of their own actions and understandings but often as shaped in relation to the ritual authority encoded within normative hierarchies and centers.

Taken together, Dalit religions are not about the unambiguous interdependence between the highest and the lowest castes and more about expressions of power and enunciations of struggle. The distinct dispositions of these faiths have far exceeded exclusive preoccupations with ritual hierarchy and/or normative authority. At the same time, however, such tendencies have been accompanied by articulations of Dalit religions with unequal relationships and ritual power at the core of caste to reconfigure these on the margins of the social order. These tangled, tension-ridden processes have defined Dalit identities, resistance, and solidarities as well as their submission, vulnerability, and subordination.

Gender and Kinship

From birth through death, the rites of passage among Dalit castes can suggest lesser and greater concern with ritual purity. Karin Kapadia argues that among the Dalit Paraiyar caste in southern India the puberty rituals occasioned by a girl's first menstruation show marked differences from the upper-caste concern with the pollution/purification of the menstruating woman: instead such rites involve quintessentially non-Brahman attempts to safeguard "the precious, distinctively female ability to create children," and to symbolically construct fertility as sacred female power. The implication is that pollution motifs are less important for Dalits (Kapadia 1995).

In contrast, another account precisely of a Paraiyar woman, Viramma, reveals more ambivalent and earthy orientations to normative purity-pollution, dominant-caste authority, and female sexuality. It is not only that the Dalits' elaborations of purity/impurity and auspiciousness/inauspiciousness entail varied negotiations of shifting arrangements of caste and power. It is also that even when certain Dalit groups closely follow the rules governing purity-pollution – during rites of birth and death, for example – they do so by conjoining such observances with the distinctive symbols and practices of their own castes and sects (Viramma et al. 1997).

Marriage and gender among Dalits have been characterized with practices such as secondary marriages for men and women, widow remarriage, the payment of a bride-price (rather than dowry), and bodily freedom from physical seclusion. Yet such arrangements have been themselves embedded in wider patterns of patrilineal kinship and their regional manifestations. Together, this has meant that Dalit women have often possessed a degree of autonomy to negotiate hierarchical relationships of kin, community, marriage(s), and motherhood. Also, their physical labor has been positively valued, practically and symbolically.

At the same time, Dalit women have evidently not escaped the asymmetries of gender and caste and the inequalities of ritual and class. Such patterns have extended from widespread depictions of the deviant sexuality of Dalit women through to their sexual and economic exploitation by upper-caste men through to attempts at controlling their bodies and labor within their communities.[27] Within these overlapping and constraining movements, the apprehensions and actions (and desires and insubordinations) of Dalit women have provided their own twists to Dalit religions and life-cycle rituals as well as wider gender arrangements and caste hierarchies.[28]

Coda

In tune with the rest of this book, the emphases of this chapter militate against principally intellectualizing, relentlessly scholastic cerebral endeavors. Instead, they indicate that my unraveling of anthropological archives – including, as disciplines of modernity – in order to rethink Dalit religions and their critical implications have their reasons. These are better posed as a question. Might my provocations modestly participate in discussions of distinct registers of religion, politics, and their interplay, including the ferment today in Dalit-Bahujan intellectual and activist endeavors, which are of course formatively about power? Far away from seeking to be the last word, mine is an attempt at conversations. Such conversations are neither empty nor fruitless. They are affective, intellectual, and embodied. They are political, aesthetic, and immanent. Conversations have consequences. Dialogues also have their gratifications.[29] For, in the end, dialogues, difficult dialogues, are necessary for what remains of our shared humanity, under terrible peril today.

Notes

1 Dedicated to the memory of DR Nagaraj, who welcomed and sustained my early engagements with Dalit worlds, always with an open spirit, intellectual generosity, creative disagreement, and warm friendship.
2 As would soon become clear, there are reasons behind my using the term Dalit "religions" as well as doing so in inverted commas. Henceforth, the inverted commas should be taken as read. This endeavor had its formal beginnings as an International Centre Goa (ICG) Lecture, titled "Rethinking Dalit Religions," delivered in January 2018. The Lecture was organized by ICG jointly with Goa University's DD Kosambi [Visiting] Chair in Interdisciplinary Studies, of which I was the occupant between 2017 and 2019. I am grateful to the ICG and Goa University. The chapter is sustained by my meandering conversations, joyful exchanges, and focused discussions across the years with Savi Sawarkar. Three other comrades and co-conspirators, Ajay Skaria, Indrani Chatterjee, and Anupama Rao provided imaginative inputs and critical comments.
3 Taken together, all that I have stated so far couldn't be further from that endless opposition between a religious India and a secular Europe. Instead, I approach religion and politics – together with identity and modernity – as contradictory, checkered, and contended processes of meaning and power. At stake are historical procedures over the past 500 years of dominance and dissonance as variously making and unmaking the modern world: protocols of modernity whose hetero-temporal-spatial coordinates have been englobed and articulated while remaining out of joint with themselves. These propositions are elaborated – in critical conversation with a wide range of writings – in Dube (2017a).

4 Bearing such ferment in mind, in this chapter I cite only necessary, indicative references, without any claims to be exhaustive. Also, I have also retained some of the style of the talk that the endeavor began as.

5 Equally, it is important to keep in view the formative heterogeneity of the scholarship that preceded such ferment. Indicative works include, for instance, Sekhar Bandyopadhyay (1997); Robert Deliège (1997); Saurabh Dube (1998, 2004a); James M. Freeman (1979); Christophe Jaffrelot (2003, 2005); Mark Juergensmeyer (1982); Ravindra S. Khare (1984); Ramdas Lamb (2002); Owen M. Lynch (1969); David N. Lorenzen (1995); Oliver Mendelsohn and Marika Vicziany (1998); Gail Omvedt (1994); Vijay Prashad (2000); and Gyan Prakash (1990). Such prior tendencies have been accessed and exceeded in more recent writings, which also bear critical plurality. Consider, for example, Badri Narayan (2006, 2011); Chinnaih Jangam (2017); Ramnarayan S. Rawat (2011); Rupa Viswanath (2014); Nathaniel Roberts (2016); Ramanarayan S. Rawat and K. Satyanarayana (2016); and Dwaipayan Sen (2018).

6 Unsurprisingly, on occasions, all of this finds linkages with concerns of turf and tenure in academic arenas.

7 It should be clear that I do not approach Dalit religions in terms of metaphysical considerations. Indeed, in scholarly literature the reference to a Dalit "metaphysics" is to be found principally – if tangentially – in the recent writing of Aniket Jaaware (2018), where he approaches the issue in Husserlian terms of a presence that claims transcendence, and which is to be laid bare through phenomenological practice, immanent reading. Basing himself on touch/not-touching and sociality/sociability at the core of caste, Jaaware raises intriguing issues of embodiment and affect, which I cannot do justice to here.

8 I am elaborating ideas first offered in Dube (1998) considering the salience of "critical margins" in opening and unraveling dominant terms of history, caste, religion, and power. See also, Dube (2004a).

9 It is in these ways, too, that I appreciate the interventionist and activist aspect of contemporary critiques of Dalit subjugation as founded in a somewhat uniform, dystopian Brahmanical ideology and practice. But I wonder also if there might not be some place for a conversation that stays with yet thinks through the demands of institutionalized politics by equally registering other claims of caste and power on Dalit subjects? It is toward such dialogue that I have presented the pressing implications of ritual articulations, layered connections, critical contentions, spatial-temporal expressions, religious attributions, and historical formations of caste and power for Dalit subjects – not only in Hinduism but within Islam, Christianity, Sikhism, and other faiths in South Asia.

10 In understandings of caste, for the total dismissal of anthropological apprehensions of religion and ritual at the behest of an analytic that is based in political-economy and the state, see, for example, Sumit Guha (2014). While there is much to be learned from Guha's work, I prefer to do so by approaching political-economy and ritual, state and religion, and power and culture in ways that think through and look beyond ready and received framings of these categories and processes. From another end, while I appreciate several of the theoretical challenges posed by Guru

and Sarukkai (2012), I am troubled by their over-drawn contrast between Western theory and indigenous experience.

11 Thus, the pain and broken-ness embodied in the signifier Dalit interrogates the paternalist loftiness of "Harijan" and the categorical governmentality of "Scheduled Castes." None of this is to deny that Dalit has a specific history, of its location and locution, its iteration and expression. Indeed, I am acutely aware of contended notations of self-description that emerged before (not merely chronologically, but as alongside and feeding into) the figure of the Dalit among vernacular publics. Such is the case, for instance, with the creation of the Satnami caste-sect in Chhattisgarh (Dube 1998); the formation of Mahima Dharma in Orissa (Banerjee-Dube 2007), and the poetics and politics of vernacular languages, subaltern publics, and everyday idioms in different parts of India going back at least to the thirteenth century (Lorenzen 1995; Novetzke 2016). The point holds as well for the crisscrossing genealogies of the emergence of the term *Acchut*, as noun and adjective, as part of Dalit endeavors and struggles in early twentieth century north India, which have been ably tracked by Ramnarayan S. Rawat (2015). To use the term Dalit, as I do in this book, exactly admits of such contentions and heterogeneities as lying at the core of identities and their politics, including attempts to variously appropriate distinct caste identities unto "reformist" Brahmanical Hinduism, evangelical Christianity, and vernacular conjunctions of Christianity and Hinduism (Dube 1998).

12 Now, such scholarly and commonplace positions go back a few centuries and extend into the present. They include, to take a few distinct examples, the emphases of the Abbé Dubois, Joan Mencher, and Kanchah Ilaiah (the last on Dalit-Bahujan religions) as well as urgent assertions that have cropped with regularity on Facebook. These emphases, including the views of the Abbé Dubois, were very well surveyed by Moffatt (1979: 6–24). See also, Mencher (1974) and Ilaiah (1996). The dispositions having become rather more routine in contemporary work on Dalits. See, for instance, Viswanath (2014). Consider also that several recent writings, including some cited earlier, whether on "structure" or "history," are impelled by the idea of Dalit (and Bahujan) "exclusion" and "separation" because they are undergirded by the ethos, ethics, and epistemology of "movements," principally in the image of Ambedkarite endeavors.

13 For an able bibliographic survey see Krause (1988).

14 In this regard, I find especially instructive the emphases of Nicholas Dirks (1989), who seeks to find the institutions and imaginaries of an "original" caste, prior to colonial presence and outside Islamic influence.

15 The labor of imperial administration and governance are often glossed today as "colonial modernity," even "colonial governmentality," buzz-terms that I find unconvincing, obfuscating, and unproductive. This should be clarified by my emphases elaborated ahead.

16 Such portrayals have become intellectual-political *doxa*, embedded not only in certified scholarship but a constituent of liberal-radical common-sense. Indeed, I doubt if cluttering this chapter with references would serve any purpose.

17 The suggestion is not that these changes happened on the same scale and in uniform ways across the subcontinent. Rather, I am pointing toward the significance of transformations of political-economy and the salience of mutations of power as jointly redefining caste in the colonial period. Indeed, it is by keeping in view such emphases that the heterogeneities of caste formations in different regions of the subcontinent – as intimated in the work of Hiroshi Fukuzawa (1991: 91–113), for instance – can assume further shape and sense.

18 For reasons of space, I mention only three salient studies, whose emphases I have rearranged toward my arguments. First, the critically imaginative, profoundly "revisionist," and enormously suggestive synthetic provocations offered by Chris Bayly (1988) over three decades ago. Second, the elaborations of several related issues by Ishita Banerjee-Dube (2015) short years back. Finally, Neeladri Bhattacharya's (2018) remarkable, wide-ranging, recent historical account – informed by critical anthropology, cultural geography, and social theory – a study whose implications I am still thinking through. It is in the light of these and related works that I have rethought my own articulation of the archives on political-economy and caste-power in Chhattisgarh in the pre-colonial and colonial eras, realizing that these annals can allow accounts with other twists, varied textures (Dube 1998).

19 I must acknowledge here the critical insights of Ajay Skaria (1999) at once on "wildness" and "caste," arguments that have yet to find sustained elaboration in the work of other scholars.

20 I am bracketing here the strenuous exorcism and simultaneous transubstantiation by Nick Dirks (2002) – and others of his ilk – that turn the imperial imagination of caste into the Indian practice of caste.

21 As was hinted earlier, especially important here are the consequences of Dr. Ambedkar's politics deriving from his position that discrimination against "untouchables" constituted the very core of caste, which led to his rejection of all claims to Hinduism in 1935. Further, since the 1960s there has been the growth of a vigorous Dalit consciousness and creativity in literature and art drawing on experiences of religious disabilities and widespread discrimination. In the twenty-first century, as we know, the terms of a Dalit politics are being carried forward through, for example, the claims of Dalit women, the forms of Dalit Christian theology, and mobilizations and campaigns for Dalit human rights, which adduce parallels between injustices of caste and wounds of race, not only in South Asia but in the Dalit diaspora and before a global public. My point is that the contending articulations of Dalit religions with ritual authority, caste hierarchy, and political power are attributes not only of the past but formative of the present.

22 Considering the emphasis on critical variations in these terrains see Jodhka (2004). See also, Carswell (2013).

23 I shall not trivialize the embodied and affective, visceral and vital experience of *being* Dalit with scholarly references in this section. Instead, I wish to acknowledge my early intimations of such exclusion and inclusion as a child of anthropologist parents who were born Brahmans but acutely opposed caste in the vernacularly modern and provincial university town,

Sagar in central India. Later, such implications came alive in itineraries of field work, archival research, but above all in the exact business of living. The anger and passion – embedded in words and expressed as images – of Savi Sawarkar sustain my writing.

24 These restrictions and exclusions derive not only from formations of purity-impurity but also those of ritual dominance of kingship and the dyad of the auspicious-inauspicious, variously tying in with processes of colonial cultures and postcolonial politics. Consider now why Dalits have not been allowed the use of umbrellas, palanquins (*palkis*), or elephants. After all, there is nothing that bespeaks purity and pollution in the case of these signifying objects. The point is that the umbrella is like a royal canopy, and the elephant is a regal mode of transport as is the palanquin. Here, the ritual dominance of kingship came together with notions of the purity-pollution and auspicious-inauspicious in the shaping of caste and power. And so too, when the Bahujan Samaj Party (BSP) uses the elephant as its electoral symbol, this is not random, there is something profoundly symbolic and substantive about the challenge. Nor should it be surprising that, more than a hundred years before the BSP, the second Satnami Guru, cast as a conqueror, not only rode on an elephant but also wore a *janeu* (sacred thread) and affirmed his authority through colonial writing. This underscores my point about the intermeshing of purity-pollution (*janeu*), ritual kinship (elephant), and colonial power (imperial writing), now expressed through the challenge to these formations of meaning and power (Dube 1992).

25 The wider implications of such displacements, negotiations, and interrogations are especially elaborated by Novetzke (2016).

26 Related emphases are expressed within the popular religious formation of Mahima Dharma of Orissa (Banerjee-Dube 2007).

27 While I am drawing upon the discussion of these themes in my own work, their implications are rather wider (Dube 2013a).

28 It bears emphasis that such patterns – from regional variations through to historical transformations and onto gendered distinctions – of Dalit religions within Hinduism also hold for other faiths. I would submit here that Dalit formations within Christianity, Islam, and Sikhism in South Asia might be usefully explored along the lines suggested by this chapter. This includes attention to how *ajlaf* Muslims, converted from Dalit and other lower castes, have distinctively understood and practiced Islam, especially by vigorously participating in popular religious traditions such as the cults of saints whose veneration cuts across religions. Similarly, the Dalits who became Sikh have created specific faiths that combine their understandings of the official doctrines and purity norms of Sikhism with popular practices of Hinduism and Islam. Finally, Dalit (and Adivasi) Christians have drawn on their membership of Orthodox and Protestant Churches to retain yet rework prior practices and wider principles of caste and worship as well as ritual and kinship, creating distinct forms of a religious identity and a vernacular Christianity, including novel representations and venerations of Hindu deities and Christian divinities where the one can complement but equally oppose the other. Joel Lee (2018) provides an able bibliography of the work on caste and Dalits in Indian Islam; on

Dalit Sikhs see, for example, Raj Kumar Hans (2016: 131–154); and on the terms of a Dalit Christianity see, for instance, Sathianathan Clarke (1998); Dube (2004a, 2010); and Zoe C. Sherinian (2014).

29 Thus, I strongly feel that something of the greatest recognition of my entire body of work – and not just on Dalits – came from the invitation to write in a special issue on Dalit feminism in the Hindi journal S*treekal*. Eventually, I wrote a long paper on gender, myth, and ritual among the Satnamis, see Dube (2013a).

4 Subjects of Privilege

Entitlements and Affects in Plutocratic Worlds

This chapter derives from a larger project constructing a historical anthropology of entitlement and privilege, as bound to capital and class as well as gender and difference – in neoliberal and nationalist times, framed by plutocratic and populist temporalities. The exercise has assumed a particular shape in its present incarnation, also putting its own spin on disciplines of modernity as well as on emergent archives.

Overture

As was noted in the Introduction, the wider study began as an ethnography and history of my high school cohort, the class of 1979, of Modern School, a co-educational institution embodying an elite status, situated in the heart of New Delhi. Since then, the exercise has expanded to include varied encounters with power-brokers, hedge-fund managers, investment bankers, and crony capitalists; alongside sustained interactions with journalists, bureaucrats, publicists, and lawyers; and back to academics and acquaintances within intellectual and everyday worlds that I routinely inhabit.

Now, over the last two decades, there has been a critical rethinking of that staple of sociological (and political) studies, the elites (e.g., Khan 2010; Mears 2011; Hay 2013; Sherman 2017; Cousin et al. 2018; Jodhka and Naudet 2019; see also, Khan 2012; Davis and Williams 2017).[1] Such shifts in sociology have been accompanied by connected efforts in related disciplines, turning for instance on anthropologies of elites (Shore and Nugent 2002; Ho 2009; Abbink and Salverda 2013; see also Ortner 2003) and new histories of capitalism (Moreton 2010; Sklansky 2012; Levy 2014; Beckert and Desan 2018; see also, Mihm 2009; Hyman 2012). My study draws upon these developments, yet with its own emphases, based on extended and intermittent fieldwork

DOI: 10.4324/9781003347569-4

over the past several years – chiefly in India, but also in the US, the UK, and Canada – alongside the use of a questionnaire and Facebook, archival materials and public histories, internet resources and contemporary reportage.[2]

Considering the diverse ways of approaching and understanding elites and their worlds, my exploratory endeavor focuses on enactments of entitlement, renderings of memory, performances of privilege, economies of affect, usages of capital, and their attendant genealogies. I do this through a critical-descriptive bid that interleaves and layers ethnographic tales, analytical emphases, and anecdotal theory. Such sensibilities are reflected also in the style, structure, and substance of this chapter, which interweaves sociological snapshots, everyday encounters, and anthropological vignettes – combining concept and narrative.[3]

Together, these emphases and procedures have two further corollaries concerning disciplines and archives, bearing upon the wider terms of this book. On the one hand, at stake throughout the chapter is the making of emergent archives, known and unknown, tattered yet textured. On the other hand, the pervasive distinctions, discussed earlier, shoring up disciplines of modernity now assume a new guise as the modern subjects' claim to surpass "traditional" hierarchies of caste and gender are haunted precisely by such palpable institutions and imaginaries, at once past and present, phantasm and future.

Spectral Starts

After India gained Independence from colonial rule in 1947, a "mixed" economy was introduced in the following decade. This entailed state control of strategic industries and infrastructural development as well as public sector corporations guiding investment, on the one hand, and a private sector of retail, trade, and non-strategic industrial production, on the other. At the same time, beginning with the Industrial Development Regulation Act of 1951, there was heavy regulation on industry, particularly licensing restrictions on those segments involved in the manufacture of industrial machinery, telecommunications, and chemicals. Such a scheme of "licence Raj" – as it came to be derogatively named – was accompanied by high tariffs and import licensing that hindered or prevented foreign goods from reaching the Indian market. Unsurprisingly, the Indian currency, the rupee, was inconvertible and the trade policy was based on "import substitution industrialization," relying on internal markets (and not international trade) for economic development.[4]

And what of agriculture? Here, landed property remained in private hands. While the state sought to carry out land reforms, especially by breaking up large "feudal" land-holdings and giving back land to the tillers, most of these efforts were subverted. Growth in agricultural production from the 1950s onwards was accompanied by periodic food shortages such that grain had to be procured from other nations, including especially the US; and the boom in certain rural regions through the "green revolution" as based on fertilizers and pesticides has been followed by intense environmental degradation as well as the substitution of basic food crops for cash crops.

At any rate, the point now is that such developments underlay the formations of the three principal dominant proprietary classes in the political economy of India: the country's richer farmers; the big business houses; and the higher-level bureaucracy. While the richer farmers, including erstwhile landlords, blocked the land to the tiller initiative, several bureaucrats "earned rents on the license and permits that were set up, in part, to protect the country's limited industrial base against domestic and foreign competition" (Corbridge et al. 2013: 124). By the 1980s, these groups had been joined by various mercantile interests, the middle peasantry, and the upper echelons of labor. All these constituencies were opposed to the liberalization of the Indian economy.

And yet liberalization occurred, beginning in 1991–1992, turning on the "deregulation of the economy, the liberalization of industry and trade, and the [gradual] privatization of state-owned enterprises" (Ganti 2014: 91). The debt crisis facing India in the early 1990s, the "rule of experts," the diffusion of dissent by adroit politics, and the incorporation of the dominant proprietary groups and class interests in policy and program that underlay the reform make for fascinating, much contended, narratives, but ones that need not detain us here. Rather, I seek to briefly uncover a more subterranean story of the shift from postcolonial development to neoliberal capitalism from the mid-1970s to the mid-1990s.

In June 1975, in the midst of rising dissent, an economic crisis, and an adverse judicial verdict against her personal misuse of the official machinery, Prime Minister Indira Gandhi of the Congress Party declared a state of national Emergency. Civil liberties were suspended, critics imprisoned, and the press censored in the exercise of authoritarian rule, especially through the command over the parliament, the judiciary, the administration, the police, and mass media. The political excesses of the Emergency years (1975–1977) are well known, including a scandalous campaign of forced sterilization toward population control – a policy backed in India by the World Bank and the IMF – and also the violent displacements of urban Muslims. At the same time, the emergent changes in political economy initiated in the period are often occluded. If this critical conjuncture was something of a pre-history of the Indian middle-class (Rajagopal 2011), it was also in these years that key conjunctions were established between salient figures in political economy and the highest echelons of political power. Effectively, in return for favors – such as freedom from licenses and absolute advantage over rivals – immense sums of money were surreptitiously made over by a chosen captain of industry to the apex of authority, the transactions conducted by the most loyal and trustworthy of lieutenants in the Congress party.[5] Such sums variously consolidated the cult of personality of a leader and the first family in control over the party, its cadre, and electoral calculations. There was now no distinction between the fortunes of the Congress party and its supreme leader, who commanded absolute loyalty, following the dissolution of inner-party democracy and the whittling of a principally "independent" civil service to turn it into a bureaucracy "committed" to the single source of power.

Indira Gandhi lost the elections held after the Emergency in 1977, and remained out of power till 1979. At the same time, the developments sketched above had wide implications. First, the exact contradictions of the coalition-based Janata government (1977–1979) not only meant a growing consolidation of mercantile and middle-peasant formations, but also uneasy openings to business interests, including as a counter to the Indira Congress's official socialist stance. Second, after Indira Gandhi and the Congress returned to power the subterranean openings to capital continued, including through links to Volkswagen and Suzuki in the building of the "people's car" in the early 1980s. Third and finally, as critical scholarship has variously revealed, the decade of the 1980s not only saw positive results in the economy – from agriculture to industry, trade to labor – but also that there were attempts at liberalization particularly in the mid-1980s as led by Rajiv Gandhi (Indira Gandhi's older son who come to power after his mother's assassination in 1984), which were defeated by dominant interests.

Now, it is exactly such contentious shifts in Indian political economy after the mid-1970s that are exorcised in the magical narrative, the tendentious tale, of reform and rupture of liberalization beginning in the 1990s, shored up by the Midas of the market and the enchantments of GDP-growth. At the same time, rather than simply demystify as mere mythology this heroic coming-of-age story of the liberalized Indian economy, it is possibly more important to register its attributes that

are constitutive of social worlds. This move turns the apparent rup-
tures of liberalization as at once a foil and a mirror in order to tell
other tales.

On the one hand, in the next section, I provide a quick sketch of
my cohort (and school) in order to delineate the uncertain unraveling
of postcolonial development as it begat neoliberal capitalism. Here,
my cohort has straddled this transition, with its childhood and adolescence as permeated by postcolonial development and desires, and
its youth and adulthood as first intimating and then inhabiting neoliberal capitalism, each in their Indian avatar. On the other hand,
in the substantive sections of the essay that follow, to be found are
subjects – from my cohort and otherwise – who principally endorse
the official account of liberalization, the enticements of neoliberalism,
and the magic of the market.[6] Yet, far from being mere phantasms of
neoliberal imaginaries, these are not even strictly neoliberal subjects.
Among the salient beneficiaries of a liberalizing regime, before and
after its formal inauguration on the subcontinent, these subjects have
distinctly shaped and stamped neoliberal capitalism in India through
their privileges and prejudices, affects and entitlements, corruption
and cronyism.

The School, the Cohort, and Other Protagonists

Modern School, Barakhamba Road, New Delhi is an intriguing institution and a known entity. Its establishment and articulation, past
and present are intimately tied to the many expressions of empire
and nationalism, the nation-state and the citizen-subject. The school
was established in 1920 by a few prominent Indian denizens of the
imperial capital as an institution that combined "modern," Western
education with "traditional," Indian values – at once straddling and
conjoining the antinomies of modernity. As chiefly a co-educational
day-school, albeit with a boarding house for boys, Modern School
has been ever associated with the power, business, and cultural elite
of the capital city. At the same time, the children of the professional
middle-classes have equally been a mainstay of the institution. In the
post-independence era, these class-constituents of the school have severally endorsed dominant nationalisms, from Nehruvian socialism to
authoritarian populism to liberalized growth to neoliberal capitalism.

Finally, Modern School has for long accepted a fair number of
"merit scholars." In our times, qualifying on economic-means bases,
generally out of lower middle-class backgrounds, these students won
scholarships after taking a rigorous examination. The merit scholars

were yanked away from their families, plucked from their neighborhoods, and placed in the boarding by way of a total immersion in the
public-school way of life. To all of us who stayed in boarding, the experience of school was marked by what was another modern, a decidedly
vernacular modern, one that articulated the virtues of postcolonial
development.[7]

My cohort from Modern School is a curious creature, especially
considering not its *representative* but its *exemplary* nature.[8] Together,
the cohort's somewhat over 200 members, one-fourth (around 50)
of whom live in the diaspora, are bearers of uncanny histories. Of
encountering adolescence exactly as we witnessed the severely authoritarian Emergency years (1975–1977) in ways that can resonate in the
depoliticized yet authoritarian orientations toward corruption, politics, and the poor today. Of growing up in routine worlds of black and
white TV – color came to us in 1982 – only to anticipate through career
choices the terms of a liberal-global economy a full decade before its
official opening in India in the early 1990s. Of being shaped by sport,
the ethic of competition, the importance of winning, to become formidable players in magical markets, assured alchemists of unfettered
capital, dizzy consumers of unbound commodities, in the midst of
crony-casino capitalism.

Inserted early into the stirrings of a neoliberal order, the cohort
includes now at least a dozen hedge-fund managers and finance capitalists, between them managing some billions of dollars, and only
half that number of civil servants, themselves not necessarily averse
to the discrete charms of capital. Medical doctors abound of course,
as do chartered accountants and engineers. At the same time, several
engineers acquired management degrees (MBAs) to join the corporate
world, many accountants started their own corporate enterprises, and
most doctors are not only in private practice but part of corporate hos-
pitals. Unsurprisingly, prior businesses have exponentially expanded
and new ones have taken off. All told, for a significant section of the
class of 1979, wealth is the principal currency of achievement. Yet,
there is an ambivalent place also for the cultural capital commanded
by the filmmakers, artists, and academics. As students of a school
ever redolent with power in the capital city, my cohort became aware
of openings in the economy and the churnings in politics from 1977
onwards, many grasping implicitly that money and capital – more
than nation and development – were the horizon for the future.

To be sure, not all from the class of 1979 have been successful. Competition and envy simmer and contention and disdain abound, especially under dispensations of capital, consumption, and corruption.

The point is that my cohort today appears formidably constituted by its inner contentions and contradictions – as, indeed, do the elites and the entitled at large – entailing at once performances of privilege, patterns of heterogeneity, invocations of unity, and claims on friendship. Unsurprisingly, all of this has been loudly evident in the sociability and jollification at the parties that frequently bring together different parts of the cohort, but also inform the quieter meetings with my class fellows.

And what of those other subjects of entitlement, not from my cohort, that populate this study? The industrialists, finance-capitalists, and power-brokers who haunt central Delhi, often provided more colorful stories – of deal-making and crony-capitalism, of masculinities and sexualities – than did my cohort. Most of these men, from their mid-fifties into their mid-sixties, were joined – individually and in groups – for walks in the Lodhi Gardens, a playground of the powerful and the rich in the Indian capital. In a few cases, they were met over breakfast, lunch, dinner, or a party, but only rarely at their homes. At the same time, the journalists and academics, publicists and civil servants, and connoisseurs and critics of art have been principally encountered at the India International Centre (IIC) in New Delhi, during my stays there of several weeks, even up to three months, every year over the past decade. These meetings could follow or precede talks and concerts; they took place over coffee or lunch, a short walk and a drink at the bar, with conversation turning principally on politics and the arts. If the site of the IIC itself embodies entitlement and privilege, I have been attentive in these colloquies to quiet claims upon innate good "taste" – especially, of accidental yet inveterate "aesthetes" – as well as to pervasive expressions of "scholasticisms" concerning personal judgments and public worlds.[9]

Key Queries

It is not just clusters of connected constituents but congeries of critical questions that I now draw upon. To begin with, rather than assuming that the "elites" connote a unified, *a priori* category as well as a constituency possessed of innate agency – as contrasted with the poor and their structural constraints, for instance (Cousin et al. 2018: 227) – my interest lies in differently articulating the notion. I approach the term "elite" as a necessarily open-ended yet critical optic-analytic as well as a doubled-edged yet multiple-hued narrative resource-technique. It only follows that while learning from social-scientific writings on the elite, my study is better approached as a historical ethnography of

entitlement and privilege, their performances and persuasions, especially as constitutive of elites and elite-ness, entangled with affect and
memory, ensnared in hierarchy and friendship, and shot through with
critical difference, particularly of the labor of gender and the specter
of caste.

Unsurprisingly, the project addresses key questions of variations
among elites, their internal contentions, their key divisions, and their
relationship with social structure (Cousin et al. 2018) in specific ways.
Here, the focus on a distinct cohort allows me to chart the issues
raised above as bound to the changing relationship between more
recent, ever emergent enactments of elite status and prior, poignant
(upper-)middle-class imaginaries as well as to the very membership
of the school as a symbol and substance of shared entitlement and
privilege. At the same time, as mentioned, I have expanded my canvas to include other claimants to elite-ness and entitlement: from
short encounters with power brokers and major capitalists; through
to sustained interactions with journalists, bureaucrats, and publicists
(building on my earlier associations); and onwards to acquaintances,
friends, and other subjects of academic and intellectual, social and
political, intimate and public worlds that I usually inhabit. The many
faces, colors, and smells of privilege are crucial to tracking the distinctions and differences, the contradictions and contentions among
the elite.

Taken together, under discussion are the ways in which affect and
entitlement, friendship and privilege, and memory and hierarchy
come together and fall apart, frequently becoming and begetting as
well as occasionally defying and disrupting each other. The tracking
of such pathways, it seems to me, is better served by weaving together
narrative and analysis, ethnographic vignettes and anecdotal theory.
This involves conjoining field materials, survey results, public histories, and contemporary reportage – in both this chapter and the larger
project on which it is based. Indeed, rather more than the pasts of my
cohort, it is the present framings of elite subjects that are the principal
concerns in the pages ahead. Ever cognizant of the incessant interplay
between power and difference, authority and alterity, at the core of
my interpretive bid are critical queries, which I briefly delineate now.

Critical Conjunctions

In a recent essay, discussing the developments in the anthropological
discipline in the midst of the long shadow cast upon it by neoliberal capitalism since the 1980s, Sherry Ortner (2016) sets up a contrast between

two tendencies: on the one hand, anthropologies of the "dark," focusing on power, domination, oppression, inequality, and their dimensions/experiences; on the other hand, studies of the "good," focusing on happiness, morality, and the ethical as well as good life. Finding much of value in each, she nonetheless endorses a third development, an ethnographically and critically reinvigorated study of "resistance," including activism and critique, as a distinct "anthropology of the good." Learning as usual from Ortner's insights, I would nonetheless like to pursue the ways in which the task of close understanding might also be to unravel the mutual interplay of power (the "dark") and difference (the "good"). For, at stake are acute anxieties of authority and intimate inflections of power, entailing the disruptions of difference and the interruptions of alterity (Dube 2004a, 2010, 2017a). To trace such resonances and dissonances is to track the incessant entanglements between entitlement and affect, to stay longer with corporeal, affective, sensuous forms of experience and knowledge, as was noted in the Introduction.

And so too we need to stay longer with Ortner (2016), in order to register that longing and loss, the sensitive and the sensuous, affect and embodiment are frequently rendered today as attributes of the ethical life, or as anthropologies of the "good." At the same time, how might such immanent attributes of social life be drawn into descriptions of entitlement and explorations of the entitled, what Ortner (2016) deems as anthropologies of the "dark"? Or, must studies of privilege and the privileged veer principally toward a "sense-less science" (Fabian 2000: ix), such that power appears as a distant enemy, even a dystopic totality (Dube 2004a, 2010, 2017a), and entitlement is left curiously bereft of its intimacies, affects, and embodiments, including in the life of the scholar, the intellectual, the writer, and the artist?

All of this suggests inter-related interpretive sensibilities. To begin with, a project that began as a study of my own cohort questions the usual distinctions between subject and object, observer and observed, and analyzer and analyzed. Now, the intimacies of studying one's own earlier habitations are not new to the study of elites (Khan 2010; Mears 2011; Cousin et al. 2018: 238–239; see also, Ortner 2003). Arguably, the twist I provide to the tale lies in my querying privilege and entitlement without readily splitting apart the academic arenas that I inhabit from the subjects of my study and their worlds. After all, I am not just the analyst but one among the subjects of the project, and so too do I wish to hold up a mirror to the conceits and entitlements, hierarchies and privileges, of intellectual cultures. Rather than those safe, hermetically sealed worlds of scholarship conjured by academics, what might be the complicities between different performances of elite-ness, including their/our participation in escalating forms of everyday dispossession?

To raise such issues is to query the conceits of a meaning-legislative reason that turns the subjects of its enquiry into objects of the analysts' self-consciousness. Instead of ready critique of distant enemies, I seek to render my cohort and other bearers of elite-ness as subjects of/with distinct reasons, with their particular logics and techniques, palpable predilections and persuasions. It follows from this that the purpose of the project is not to pointedly demystify social worlds and their inhabitants, but to critically affirm and cautiously question these terrains and subjects in order to unravel their textures, terms, and transformations (Dube 2004a, 2017a). Yet, it is to take up these tasks by registering that such interplay between meaning and power is never innocent, and lies at the core of our scandalously unequal, profoundly murky worlds. Here are to be found routine enactments of entitlement and endless enticements of privilege – turning on the spatial and the sexual, money and masculinity, caste and gender, the magical and the modern – that I now narrate through strange, even uncanny, stories.

Habitations of Hierarchy

"The value of property in [New] Delhi," a once precocious and now wise classmate told me, "derives from its nearness to 7 Race Course Road [the Indian Prime Minister's residence, and so the actual seat of state power]." Rather more than just the physical proximity to political decision-making, at stake are the mutual determinations of scarcity and value of real estate within the larger layout of the capital city. Here, it is ministers, politicians, judges, bureaucrats, and defence personnel who live in the Lutyen's Bungalow Zone (LBZ) that covers 26 square kilometers at the center of New Delhi. The LBZ is made up of around 1,000 Bungalows, of which rather less than one-tenth are privately owned. Now, in close proximity of the LBZ are neighborhoods such as Jor Bagh, Golf Links, and Sundar Nagar, where there are rather more properties to go around, also on account of the fact that here plots have been divided as property-developers raze older houses to replace them with four-story constructions that have an apartment on each floor. The prices for properties in the LBZ and its nearby neighborhoods are mind-boggling. Roughly speaking, a house on a one-acre plot (4,840 square yards/4,050 square meters) in the zone can be priced at around 600 INR crores (or 80 million USD), while in the nearby neighborhoods prices can go up to 250 INR crores (or 34 million USD) for a house on a half-acre property. Of course, these values are not only about actual prices but crucially the subject of distinct, contentious claims upon elite status.

Very soon after beginning to plan the project on my cohort I got in touch with a corporate success and rich-beyond-measure classmate in order to set up a possible meeting. I was calling from a land-line number in East Delhi, home to several group housing co-operatives where a large number of academics now live. The call was well received but also interrupted by an impatient enquiry, "What kind of a strange number are you using?" My anonymous, unknown, strange location was already a measure of social distance from the plush neighborhood that I was calling. At stake are intimations of entitlement as embodied in habitations of privilege, which together produce elite-ness within hierarchical cityscapes, suggesting the salience not only of attending to the structural properties that influence elites (Cousin et al. 2018), but of equally understanding the structured spaces that elites occupy.

Actually, I am still staggered by how many members of my cohort live in neighborhoods bordering Lutyens' Delhi, a tiny handful owning properties in the heart of the latter. If there are tales within tales of entitlement here, it is also the case that the enactments of the privilege of this set rest upon principally meeting each other, ever eschewing the middle classes. Unsurprisingly, my account of contemporary India rests on entwining the affiliations of entitlement, hierarchy, and privilege with the alignments of affect, memory, and friendship, each axes endlessly bound to the other. Put differently, affect, memory, and friendship often beget entitlement, hierarchy, and privilege, only occasionally undoing one another.

At the 30th reunion of my high school class, elegant, small tent-like, covered arrangements were set up outside the main, immense arena where the event was enacted. This was a thoughtful gesture to accommodate friends meeting after a long time who would wish to catch up away from the hullabaloo. But three members of the cohort set themselves up in one of these enclosures from the very beginning and refused to come out. As one of them announced on behalf of all the absolutely entitled, "You expect me to go inside and shake hands with these middle-class people." I am not sure how the imbroglio was resolved. Perhaps, it had something to do with moves that allowed "class" to be enacted within the class, turning upon the conjuring of classy single malt whiskey rather than cheaper Scotch, a class-act within the class-reunion. The immediate point is that these three members of the cohort all live in the most well-heeled parts of New Delhi.

Despite its drama, the tale is not an exception. Not so long ago, I was invited to a dinner in a terribly tony neighborhood. The invitees consisted chiefly of members of different classes/cohorts from the middle to the end of the 1970s of Modern School, and (in one case) their adult children (who also attended Modern School). But this was not the only connection between the guests. As one of my school seniors announced to a small group – milling close to the incredibly well-stocked bar and its liveried servers – "it is really amazing, no, that all of us live in GL [this neighborhood]." The seemingly simple statement bears wide import.

First, the innate entitlement and distinction of a group of around twenty alumni of one school, all close in age, were asserted and captured through a singular frame: their habitation of an exclusive neighborhood, embodying a poetics of privilege. Second, the evocation of this unity of entitlement – among a tiny group that yet bore disparate attributes of status and wealth – served to mark them off as a distinct entity, turning on its own axis of neighborhood, apart from those vexing middle-classes, belonging to the school, the city, and the nation at large. Finally, this performance of privilege, when placed alongside the practices of elite-ness that are embodied in the foremost neighborhoods of the capital, suggests an elite that inhabits a country of their imagi*nation* but who has also actually abdicated India. For, in this world, at its apex, "flying first-class [on commercial airlines] is so boring, no?" And if private jets are the way to go, it is a theatre, too, where a weekend in Capri, celebrating a fortieth birthday and a second divorce, involves modest outlays of around 300,000 dollars.[10] (Don't ask me how I know.)

Distinctions of Privilege

It is easy to assume that such statements, these practices, and their bearers belong principally to a *nouveau riche*. Yet, to do so would not be simply facile. It would also bring into play prior presumptions – often held by the middle-classes as well as the culturally entitled, including especially academics and intellectuals – concerning the inherent vulgarity of displaying wealth and of talking about money. After all, it is such rudeness that the "old" elite are assumed to refrain from. At stake instead are reconfigurations of class, with older privilege and political-capital finding new expressions of money and power quite as formidable subjects of novel wealth – derived from multinational corporations and capital, banking and industry, real-estate and power brokerage – come to the fore.

Far from those ready, set-in-stone distinctions between "old" and "new" elites, it is important to focus instead on the actual articulations of entitlement and elite-ness, class and capital, and power and politics, which can reveal unusual bed-fellows and register clear differences in enactments of privilege. It bears emphasis that the stories ahead are not just of the transformations of economy and capitalism but of the makeovers of the state and governance. At the same time, it is salient to stay with the ways in which earlier "indigenous" and newer "cosmopolitan" templates of being elite are drawn upon in the performance of privilege. Within the interstices of these processes – intimating projections of privilege that are necessarily context-bound – enactments of entitlement entail the quiet presence of caste and the unquiet play of gender, issues that I cannot do justice to in this chapter.[11]

Some years ago, I received a curious invitation. In the setting dusk of October in central Delhi, in the impossibly beautiful Lodhi Gardens, I was keeping pace with two tall walkers, each representing distinct ends of business interests, of consumption and capital, in the neoliberal India of public, unbridled corruption. Without warning, my principal companion, a member of my cohort, suddenly asked: "Do you want to come for a party tonight?" I demurred and deferred. Seeing my hesitation, he added, "*Waise bhi, lala log milenge* (in any case, you will meet folks only with new money [and lack of class])." This piqued my interest and I accepted the invitation with alacrity. The venue was a super-luxury hotel, but my host warned me: "Don't ask for me by name. The party will be in the name of a Mr. Agarwal." And then came the zinger, "*CBI se darr lagta hai* (I am scared of the CBI [Central Bureau of Investigation, India's premier investigative agency, which deals with economic crimes, special crimes, and high-profile and corruption cases])."

The die was cast. The darkness had descended. As we approached the end of our ramble, my companion called out to another walker – with (what seemed like) two bodyguards – in the dim distance, "*Sir, aarahe hain na aaj raat ko?* (Sir, you are coming tonight, right?)"

The party was a celebration of an event in politics and another in sport: the acquisition of important positions in both these terrains by the same person. As I reached the plush premises of the main venue in a dinky taxi, Mr. Rana, the driver, suggested that rather than pull up to the main porch, I was better off wending my way on foot between the immense cars that choked the driveway. And so I wiggled through a battery of Bentleys, Rolls-Royces, Maseratis, and other equal and slightly lesser creatures to find myself in an enormous, resplendent hall. Here were tables laden with delectable Sushi and an open bar serving top liquor, all in the midst of canned instrumental music based on old Bollywood film songs and representing (to me) monumental bad taste. Even before I met my host, I saw the gentleman with the bodyguards we had crossed earlier that evening in Lodhi Garden. Standing in a distant, quiet corner, he was being feted by the primary guests, those who could gain access to him, on his double acquisition.

My host greeted me with a sociological gem: "All these people you see here," he said with matter of fact acceptance-cum-condescension, "their money has been made in the last decade or so [since the early 2000s]." Surrounded by power-brokers – at the confluence of business and corporate interests, developers and fixers, bureaucrats and politicians – I was in the midst of worlds that have come to pass as a new age of glitter, of sophisticated bling and rude taste, formed and transformed by the products of a newly minted, gilded India.

The first person I was introduced to at the party was presented simply as "the coal-king of India." No name followed, but a description did: "He is worth 32000 crores [INR]." Having just begun to mull over the gentleman's obviously expensive yet equally unfathomable (for me) upper-garment and his principally unprepossessing exterior, I was utterly thrown, terribly confused: Didn't more than 80% of the coal industry, ever since its nationalization, lie in the hands of the public sector undertaking Coal India Limited? Wasn't 32,000 crores equal [then] to around 6,000 million USD? Wait, wasn't 6,000 million USD actually 6 billion USD? And so why was the gentleman not listed in wealth reckoning magazines such as Forbes India? Was this because he was the coal mafia, and had blood on his hands?

Even before I could start getting my head around all this, it was my turn to be introduced: Once more no name was deemed necessary – that seemed to be the way at that party – and I was merely presented as my host's friend since our school days. At this the coal king said to me, *"Arrey inhonain hummey teen saal main itna sikhaya hai to aapko tees saal main kitna sikhaya hoga?* (Now, he [my host] has taught me so much in three years how much would he have taught you [referring to me] in thirty years?)" My blood froze.

There are other stories from that party, turning on my encounters with one of the owners of an IPL (Indian Premier League) cricket franchise, a very successful administrator (and known to be terribly corrupt), the proprietor of a gymnasium – frequented by the powerful and the well-connected – in the capital, and a slinky and shifty go-between figure who kept shaking his head and clicking his fingers to the instrumental muzak. Needless to say, all this happened as major movers, serious shakers, and formidable fixers from the terrains of business and bureaucracy, of politics and performance mutually articulated the idioms and mediums of power brokerage. The point is that while the distinctions among these protagonists were recognized, they were also understood as common players in the same field.

Here to query ready invocations of absolute differences between the "old" and the "new" elite is to track instead the carving of new formations of money and elite-ness, wealth and power. After all, at stake is nothing less than the spectral state, featuring power-brokers who have not so much abdicated India as they have auctioned and bought, possessed and owned the state – not all of it of course but crucial components nonetheless.

All of this is clarified further by my other encounters, including especially in Lutyens' Delhi and nearby environs. In the Lodhi Gardens, the elites and the middle-classes – from its upper echelons through to its lower reaches – find their own companions to walk and exercise with. While some set up prior appointments, the members of most groups arrive at more or less known times and join their other companions: the walks are always on the outer track in a specified direction, clockwise or anti-clockwise. Serendipitously, sometime ago, I got to join for a few days a cabal of elite walkers, most of its members five to ten years older than me. On offer were enormously illuminating meanderings.

I was walking on my own in the Gardens in the morning when an acquaintance from the IIC called out and asked me to join his group. I was introduced to his companions as a professor in Mexico, who taught "the sexiest girls in the world." The stage was set and he now asked me: "Buddy, you had said Machu Pichu [in Peru] is really beautiful. Should I go there with my wife [an architect, who I have met at least a few times] or my girlfriend?" I suppose banter is in my blood, for I replied: "The place is lovely enough to go to twice." Far from being lost, the implications were appreciated, and I was included as an honorary fellow-traveler (before they tired of me after four walks).

Those walks contain a maelstrom of stories – and tales within tales – to which I plan to return in the near future. A few quick points shall have to suffice here. First, the elite walking group is far from being unified in terms of class background and prior status. Rather, they represent distinct trajectories in the making and unmaking of Indian capital, present and past. Consider the contrasts between two of the key constituents of the group: a first-generation real estate developer with uncertain educational qualifications, who has amassed vast holdings – based upon learning on the job and being street-smart – and himself now lives in a one acre, 600 crore INR (80 million USD) house in Lutyen's Delhi; and a scion of a venerable family – its riches, status, and influence reaching back to the past few centuries – who commands impressive educational credentials alongside the family fortune, the latter itself appropriately invigorated in more recent times. The distinctions extend to the industrialist who established himself in a hesitantly liberalizing India to command significant resources today yet whose status is principally bound to the connection of the family with having designed some of the most iconic buildings at the core of central Delhi; and to a shadowy character, the alumnus of an elite college, who appears intimate with Israel's army. Second, what binds the group is privilege, property, and power as its members walk together to perform a shared elite-ness turning upon money and masculinity, each inescapably gendered of course. Indeed, the manner of my being presented to the group was unexceptional: a pervasive, predatory sexuality is the soul and substance of conversations that cements its mutual status. Finally, age, experience, and interest(s) mean that at play among the group was not so much the terms of an uncertain abdication of the Indian nation but an easy command over the land. Once more, old wealth and new money, earlier entitlement and present privilege become and beget each other in contemporary India.

None of this is to suggest that the presence of money and the pursuit of mammon, ill-begotten or not, have dissolved all distinctions between the old and the new elite in neo-Delhi. Different forms of "boundary maintenance" matter, immensely so: indeed, each of the enactments of entitlement – whether of neighborhood or of crony-capitalism or of walking regimens – discussed above are bound by their place of performance. Here key commonalities of shared privilege are carefully cultivated, indeed even anxiously sutured, for else all might fall apart.

Long after our last meeting in high school, I was on the phone with a corporate success story from the class of '79 toward an appointment for a chat. He suggested a drink in the evening. I agreed, mentioning the bar of the India International Centre, widely considered a privileged watering-hole in the capital city. Obviously, this did not cut it. My classmate said simply, "Let us meet some place more interesting." I knew then that an intriguing encounter lay ahead, but was still not prepared for the immense black limousine that turned up to whisk me off to a terribly exclusive club – where corporate head-honchos network – of a super-luxury hotel.

Once again, the meeting produced several salient stories, which lead in distinct (albeit overlaying) directions: but I shall focus on two critical points here. On reaching the lush lounge, I found my classmate to be one of only two client-occupants of the immense arena, sitting at a table looking out toward a shimmering swimming pool. The other man, bearing a shock of red (henna-dyed) hair and wearing a flashy safari suit, was seated at some distance in a distinct, inner section of the lounge. Not much later, my classmate and I were joined by his spouse, a CEO of an important company, who I was meeting for the first time and whose elegant Indian dress – I forget now whether it was a Saree or a Salwar-Kameez – complemented her husband's expensive suit.

After introductions were made, the first round of drinks imbibed, and delicate canapes consumed, the unhurried conversation, the quiet jokes, and the unguarded laughter began to flow. Clearly, all this – alongside my polo-shirt, casual trousers, and unfamiliar use of language – piqued the curiosity of the safari-suited, red-haired gentleman. He moved to the next table, in order to better see and hear just what it is that was going on. It was a bad move. The gentleman in question might have been a full-fledged member of the club and loaded with mullah to boot, but the boundaries and breaches of class(-fractions) could not be trifled with. This newly entitled elite of "land or mining mafia," as another friend later identified his kind, was gently but firmly persuaded by an ever-alert steward to return to his earlier table. The circles of privilege stood drawn.

Here, a steward of the club was the instrument for instating the edges of entitlement. This is entirely in keeping of course with the ways in which servants, staff, and subordinates at large are critical to the performance of privilege and its hierarchies, as not only a mere backdrop but as quietly an assiduous frontline of these phenomena.[12] Unsurprisingly, too, during our time at the club, the two stewards hung to every word, gesture, and shift in comportment – of mind and body – of my classmate. They were principally respectful toward me, mildly deferential toward his spouse, and entirely obsequious toward him. As we left the club, the way was led by my classmate, the two stewards three steps behind him, and then his spouse and me. If the prime protagonist's corporeal manner – sustained and upheld now by three (small) scotch whiskeys – was visibly regal, the stewards' slightly bent bodies, smarmy demeanor, and simpering speech during the scripted walk to the club's doors reminded me of the theatrical performances of lowly courtiers toward the king or emperor in old Bollywood cinema, usually in black and white. A re-enacted royalty of corporate wealth appeared as the resonant leitmotif of entitled elite-ness in contemporary India.[13]

What then of caste, gender, and the differences they introduce among the subjects under discussion? The entitled moderns of shining India assert, implicitly if urgently, that they have superseded caste as institution and imagination. Yet the specters of caste are constitutive of their entitlement. On the one hand, the exact habitations and the very habitus of modern subjects, their claims upon cosmopolitanism and its precise privileges, decree the obsolescence of caste. This is of course in keeping with the best tradition of the "ought" triumphing over the "is." On the other hand, if entitlement is about accomplishment caste status has to be ambivalently denied yet also uncertainly accepted. After all, privilege has to follow from somewhere, including in the rare instance (involving the now entitled lower caste person) of its coming out of nowhere. The tales abound, but have to await another telling.

As also have to be deferred the detailed tales of gender, which spill from the surface to the subterranean, each binding the other. The point now is that the masculinities, the sexualities, and their anxieties, which appeared earlier, are gendered issues. The spouses of these men are not mere pawns in an unremitting, seamless patriarchy, but subjects that imbue unequal, hierarchical, entitled arenas with their spirit and substance, soul and subversion (Bhandari 2019). And so, too, the solidarities of affect and friendship among women often exceed the terms of entitlement and hierarchy – all the while accessing formations of privilege – in ways that undo the best of bonds among the men. Is it the case that key attributes of disciplines of modernity – as founded on the progressivist distinction between prior enchantments and posterior emancipations – now spill over unto quotidian clamors of the modern, its subjects claiming to have broken the shackles of "tradition" whose living specters yet continue to haunt them?

Coda

After principally studying dispossessed, marginal, and subaltern subjects for three and a half decades, can I bring such learning and unlearning to bear upon key attributes of the study of elites and suchlike? How do we understand the haunting today of the globe and the planet by the interplay between privilege and politics, entitlement and hierarchy, cronyism and friendship, injustice and indecency, and domination and dispossession? Might we approach these routine outrages not as mere errors of understanding, but as bearing corporeal, embodied, affective, sensuous, worldly attributes of economy, society, and politics that suggest issues crucial to the contemporary world? Can a critical ethnography and a contemporary history of entitlement and privilege centered principally on the Indian capital yet carry resonance for understanding larger worlds of capital and power?

As the wider project unravels, the path in front yet remains strange, even uncertain. Staying away from ready resolution much depends on the terms and textures of description, the requirements and registers of writing. Considering that cities are usually described – at least by their analysts – as utopian or dystopian if the focus is on the poor, do worlds appear paradisal or paradoxical when viewed from the perspectives of privilege, in the mirrors of their predilections, prejudices, and practices? How are we to write of dizzy, terrifying spectacles of capital and consumption, that put to shame even Walter Benjamin's Angel of History, the angel who hovers above us, his wings caught in the storm blowing from paradise, the storm that we call progress? Is not the debris of history, of progress, that the angel sees from afar even more petrifying from up close? Yet why do we shy from – and what might we endorse, when – facing up to social worlds commandeered by the entitled and the elite?

Notes

1 For lack of space, I am not recounting "classical" studies of the elite – for example, those by Vilfredo Pareto, C Wright Mills, and Pierre Bourdieu – though they continue to offer valuable lessons today.
2 Three points bear further mention. First, the fieldwork for the study has included recorded conversations with around 50 members of my cohort, ranging from one to eight hours in duration. Second, I have followed (and interacted with) several members of cohort and other subjects of this study on Facebook. Finally, contemporary reportage includes accounts such as those of Crabtree (2018), Dasgupta (2014), McDonald (1998), and Guha Thukurta et al. (2014), which are best read together with critical stories on internet and mainstream media, on the one hand, and scholarly accounts (e.g., Gupta 2017), on the other.
3 It bears emphasis that none of this is merely "postmodern" affectation. Rather, it brings together the principal tendencies in the modern human sciences over the last two centuries: the analytical, the hermeneutical, and their interplay, while querying the terms of an aggrandizing, legislative reason (see, for instance, Dube 2004a, 2010, 2017a, 2021a).
4 This section draws upon and acutely summarizes a vast variety of scholarship, which has been read over several years. Here, I cite only the most essential studies, which would also orient the interested reader to the key issues.
5 Such stories have barely circulated due to their secretive, sensitive nature. Consider that the chosen satrap in the Congress conducting shady transactions during the Emergency (and after) went onto become the President

of the Republic of India from 2012 to 2017; and that the kingpin in the chemicals industry that contributed quietly to the party sired one of the richest man in the world – and his billionaire younger brother – that have close connections with current Hindu Right government. The tales have been shared with me by truly senior journalists and ex-bureaucrats, who are also the elite subjects of this study (see also, McDonald 1998; Crabtree 2018).

6 Albeit with varied emphases, these subjects severally express neoliberalism as: (i) an economic program of deregulation, liberalization, and privatization; (ii) "a prescriptive development model" offering truly distinctive "political roles for labor, state, and capital"; (iii) an ideology that values market exchange as an absolute ethic that ought to guide human action; and (iv) "a mode of governance that embraces the idea of the self-regulating free market" as the grounds for "effective and efficient government" (Ganti 2014: 91).

7 I am providing the minimal necessary information on Modern School and my cohort here, especially as capturing the shift from postcolonial "development" to neoliberal "growth,' discussed above.

8 The social-economic background of the class of 1979 is clarified by a directory compiled by the organizers of the thirtieth reunion of the cohort; an open-ended questionnaire that I sent out to 170 members of the class and that was answered by around 100 of them; extended recorded conversations, mentioned above, with around 50 constituents of the cohort; and my wider fieldwork among them. All of these also lie at the core of the study.

9 On modern scholasticisms see the next chapter. It discusses how, abounding in public worlds as in the academy, such scholasticisms find well-deliberated statements and everyday expressions, acutely embodying and endorsing, constitutively coining and crafting – entitlement, privilege, and hierarchy.

10 On such questions of elite sociality and territorial demarcations, see Cousin and Chauvin 2013; Sherman 2017; Bruno and Salle 2018.

11 Caste is a silent signifier of *a priori* privilege (and its absence) rather than a formally constitutive resource among the subjects of this study. In other contexts, caste has been a crucial to capitalism in India.

12 This is true of all the encounters discussed so far, including the walks in the Lodhi Gardens: after all, at home and in office – and at clubs and hotels, restaurants and gyms – it is a retinue of subordinates of distinct descriptions, who actually bear the burden of the entitlement of the master. The relationship with servers and servants can extend from varieties of paternalism and no-nonsense contractual connections through to the unleashing of the most filthy, vile abuse upon them in the worst cases. Of course, there are many hues in between. At the same time, the women of the family can command the retinue in particular ways, raising critical issues of gender, which are only briefly touched upon later in this chapter. The point is that these are all questions that I propose to discuss in the wider project.

13 It is worth pursuing how this might be a variation on a theme: of templates of privilege of the ones referred to as "the one percent" as finding culturally particular manifestations. For the present, I confine myself to noting

two matters. On the one hand, the idea of a new royalty of taste has wide implications – extending beyond the elite – to identifications with celebrity and consumption: first/business-class travel, luxury cruises, and designer brands alongside exclusive hotels, restaurants, and clubs, for example. On the other hand, at least some among the immensely rich, especially those who are connected to the auction economy of power brokers and the state, can refer to themselves as *raja-log* (kingly person), laying claims on the royal figure and regal form, now of dodgy business of property and wealth. There is much to explore ahead.

5 Issues of Immanence

Modern Scholasticism and Academic Entitlement

The chapter ahead is something of a patchwork, one that stitches, layers, and pieces together common motifs of academic life and uncommon shapes of critical questions. I focus principally on considerations of (everyday) immanence and (modern) scholasticism. Yet, in doing so, I necessarily draw in attributes of the analytical and the affective as well as issues of entitlement and enquiry. The bid is at once to affirm the presence in the world of these concepts-entities *and* to unravel their constitution and contention in academic arenas. It is in these ways that I raise questions regarding earthly immanence, modern (worldly-scholastic) transcendence, and academic privilege in our own times. Needless to say, taking this book forward, the wider emphases and key implications of this chapter equally probe the hierarchical distinctions that have undergirded the disciplines of modernity, exactly as they point toward philosophy and theory as well as the everyday and the routine as archives at large.

Beginnings

Indeed, I explore here issues of earthly immanence while querying the incessant clamor of worldly-scholastic transcendence. It warrants emphasis that transcendence and immanence are usually understood in relation to the divine, based upon the antimony between enchantment and disenchantment in/of the world. As should soon become clear, querying such oppositions my emphasis is on an *earthly immanence*, which is *not* predicated upon the divine.[1] Equally, in speaking of transcendence, ever in relation to scholasticism, my reference is to assumptions of immaculate knowledge that occlude and ignore the traces and tracks of its maculate birth in the world. In a sense, then, the widest question I am asking is the following: In articulating

DOI: 10.4324/9781003347569-5

worlds of today and yesterday, can our endeavor rest upon an accept-
ance of earthly immanence rather than seek requirements of worldly-
scholastic transcendence?

At this point, it is worth staying a little longer with the terms,
modern scholasticism and worldly transcendence, which beget each
other.[2] Now, as the Introduction briefly delineated, scholasticism
commonly refers to the system and method of teaching and learning of theology and philosophy that was predominant in Europe
from the twelfth to the sixteenth centuries. Indeed, the term was
invented by sixteenth-century Renaissance humanists to pejora-
tively describe the stylistic verbosity and sterile intellectualism of
such tendencies.[3] At the same time, principally drawing on the work
of Pierre Bourdieu (1984, 2000) and conjoining this with the emphases of Jacques Rancière (1989, 1991, 2004), my use of scholasticism
has a wider purchase. Quite simply, it refers to orientations and
understandings in the past and the present that turn their particular
case into the general story while forgetting the conditions that make
this possible.

Put differently, modern scholasticisms cut across different ideological orientations and distinct political practices as part of their apprehending, objectifying, and acting upon the past, present, and future.
What is common to all of them is the formative privileging of their
own "ought" over the acute contentions, or the exact "is," of contradictory worlds, assiduously brushing aside also contending historical subjects. It is exactly such spectacular conjuring that I refer to as
worldly-scholastic transcendence.[4] Now, scholastic protocols of such
transcendence exist as dispositions and structures – or, as structured
dispositions – that are not only academic, merely intellectual, simply
philosophical. Actually, these procedures are terribly worldly. They
embody and engender entitlement, privilege, and hierarchy – of arguments and analytics, of words and worlds.

Elaborating on these propositions, my endeavor ahead is exactly
to unravel such scholasticisms and their implications by exploring
at once the conceptual conventions *and* everyday life-worlds of the
academy. It is to take up these tasks in order to track how the heterogeneous yet immaculate "ought" of modern scholasticism – and
its constant claims of worldly transcendence – formidably beget and
betoken the cultural privilege of academic arenas. Taken together, the
essay weaves together motifs, designs, and patterns that emerge from
the constant claims of worldly transcendence, scholastic reasoning,
academic entitlement, and their interplay, while registering the quiet
possibilities of earthly immanence.

Primary Stitches

Concerning the careful questioning(s) of modern knowledge as bound to the imaginative affirmation(s) of social worlds, under issue are the ways in which academic and everyday arenas come together and fall apart. This is to say that rather than bracketing and sheltering intellectual arguments from the wider worlds in which they are embedded, such claims and conceits require being constantly submitted to the demanding terms of quotidian terrains, including the mutual intimations of power and meaning, authority and alterity, the dominant and the subaltern in these domains.

Drawing upon such dispositions – while braiding together analytical impulses with hermeneutic sensibilities – my own endeavor has distinguished between historically located "subjects of modernity" as bearers of heterogeneous reasons/understandings, on the one hand, and routine representations of the "modern subject" as insinuating a singular rationality, on the other.[5] Actually, the distinction lies at the core of my understanding of modernity, which I approach not merely as an idea, an ideal, an ideology but as historical processes of meaning and power that stretch back over the past five centuries, as was discussed earlier.

The point is that to distinguish between an exclusively-rendered modern subject and necessarily-heterogenous subjects of modernity is especially salient – in historical and theoretical ways – for thinking through a pervasive meaning-legislative, adjudicatory reason that abounds in the academy while also of course extending far beyond. Indeed, such a rationality (and rationale) frames the objects it considers in the image of the commentator-analysts' singular, self-same reason rather than as subjects of other reasons, entailing equally issues of entitlement and privilege, affect and embodiment.[6]

The present chapter takes forward these concerns by narrating the persistent presence of distinct scholasticism(s) – involving the substitution of any contentious "is" by their own "ought" – in academic and everyday worlds. Indeed, I explore how these tendencies are tied to formidable conceits of knowledge-making that are variously founded on terms of transcendence, worldly yet prophetic, which come to haunt even those bids that seek to escape them. Throughout, I shall seek to unravel, if often implicitly, the place of an earthly immanence – itself tied to textures of affect and embodiment, formations of the sensuous and the political – as a means of approaching and understanding the past and present. At the end, I shall draw together these considerations by articulating anew my prior proposal (first made nearly two decades ago) of a "history without warranty."

Clearly, running through this essay is a querying of the prerogatives of scholasticisms, especially the immaculate ought they betoken and betray, in academic arenas. Here, I approach the academy as a culturally and politically layered arena, constituted by distinct formations of privilege and hierarchy, entitlements and their interrogations, which turn, for instance, on gender and caste, class and race, status and sexuality. Academic arenas can be thought of, then, as rather in the manner of an *ethnographic fields*, located in space-time, ever part of social worlds with their own quotidian cultures, in which academics work but also live. The utterances and practices of scholarly subjects, especially those of the *observer*, in everyday academic spaces – for example, seminars, cafes, bookshops, and social media – can be enormously revealing here. Such routine words and reflex gestures often reveal wider assumptions and affects, entitlements and experiences of intellectual terrains. Unsurprisingly, too, despite the repeated claims of academic arguments as being unsullied by everyday worlds, the certified statements within the academy are uncannily haunted by the mundane, its perversions and possibilities.

Indeed, the point precisely might be to *not* separate the everyday assumption and the accredited expression of intellectual endeavor. For, taken together, at stake are un-said, under-said, and already-said orientations and arguments undergirding life and understanding within academic cultures. In the pages ahead, I explore at once the quotidian manifestations and the licensed expressions of scholarly domains. It is in these ways that I also intimate, necessarily implicitly, the wider terms of privilege and their questioning in social worlds, which academic arenas embody and in which they are embedded, albeit of course in their own ways.

Unraveling Immanence

My arguments are undergirded by overlapping dispositions to academic categories and social worlds. This brings up the question: What do I mean by immanence? To start off, here is what I pit immanence against: the widespread view of the world as "disenchanted," such that the place in this world of "the value properties (good or bad, hostile or benign) that make normative demands on us" is sought be excised, indeed exorcized (Bilgrami 2010). Needless to say, such seeing has played a central role also in the conception of the world "as alien to our sensibilities of practical engagement, ... something either to be studied in a detached way or, when practically engaged with, to be engaged with as something alien, to be mastered, conquered, and controlled for our utility and gain" (Bilgrami 2010). Now, I query the presumption of such detachment and avow instead being open to "not only the words on our pages and on our lips and not only the images on our canvases, but [to] objects and things in the world, including in nature, [that] are filled with properties of value and meaning" (Bilgrami 2014: 183).[7]

At the same time, however, I hold also that the terms and textures of disenchantment bear their own enchantments, which

> ...extend from the immaculately imagined origins and ends of modernity through to the dense magic of money and markets; and from novel mythologies of nation and empire through to hierarchical oppositions between myth and history, emotion and reason, ritual and rationality, East and West, and tradition and modernity. Intensely spectral but concretely palpable, forming tangible representations and informing forceful practices, the one bound to the other, such enticements stalk the worlds of modernity's doing and undoing. The enchantments of modernity give shape to the past and the present by ordering and orchestrating these terrains, at once temporally and spatially.
>
> (Dube 2017a: 64)

Such ordering and orchestration also extend far beyond a mere detached observing of the world. Rather, we are in the face of powerful processes, embedded within pervasive projects of meaning and power, which name and objectify worlds in order to rework and remake them. Here, the antinomies and enticements of modernity become structures of sentiment and attributes of experience in the lives of subjects. Being made of the world – that is, as formidably *worlded* – these oppositions and enchantments acutely acquire value properties, which invite and incite action and contention. As we shall soon see, enormous significance is borne here by the affective, the embodied, and the extra-analytical, the everyday and the mundane, all issues/forms of immanence, which unfold on distinct registers/fabrics.

To start off, the claims that I question in this chapter and book are neither treated as ideological aberrations and mistaken practices nor cast as mere objects of knowledge, detached attributes of social worlds, awaiting simple confirmation or ready refutation. Instead, they are approached as stipulating and shoring-up the worlds we inhabit, such that these meanings and practices appear as conditions of knowing, insinuating ways of being, which require careful, critical articulation. This means further to desist from defining such propositions and

positions as principally cerebral-cognitive endeavors. It is to register rather their dense worldly dimensions, which not only name the
world but work upon the world in order to remake it. Does this possibly put another spin on the need to think through analytical categories of an academic provenance by bringing them in conjunction
with the quotidian configurations of the terrains they describe, the
resolute requirements of immanent worlds? Can this be done by neither privileging the one (the academic or intellectual) nor the other
(the everyday or mundane), but vigilantly unraveling both in view of
their critical articulation? Can such tasks be taken up while keeping
in view the insight of the radical Durkheim that it is in routine worlds
(arguably of immanence) that the unimaginable is imagined? Finally,
as was discussed earlier, in approaching and understanding academic
and everyday arenas, is it not critical to stay longer with corporeal,
affective, and sensuous modes of experiencing, being, and knowing?[8]

Motif One

Not long after the attacks of 9/11 in New York, the political theorist
Craig Calhoun was in Mexico City. At El Colegio de México, Craig
focused on "actually existing cosmopolitanism" as a "view from the
frequent-flyers lounge," raising a range of critical questions. Principally, he suggested that:

> On September 11 [2001], terrorists crashing jets into the World
> Trade Center and Pentagon ... precipitated a renewal of state-
> centered politics and a "war on terrorism" seeking military rather
> than law enforcement solutions to crime. ...One need be no friend
> to terrorism to be sorry that the dominant response to the ter-
> rorist attacks has been framed as a matter of war rather than
> crime, an attack on America rather than an attack on humanity...
> Militarism gained and civil society lost ...as the US and other
> administrations moved to sweep aside protections for the rights of
> citizens and immigrants alike and strengthen the state in pursuit
> of "security."
>
> (Calhoun 2009)[9]

Calhoun went to explore the terms of this challenge to
cosmopolitanism – through claims on technology, economy, and
ideology – whose very anti-Western impulse revealed a contending
modern project, a statist anti-modernist venture formative of modernity and its contradictions.

All reasonable provocations, one would assume, which bid us to stay with and think through our own taken-for-granted presumptions about images and worlds, especially turning on cosmopolitanism and modernity, state and citizen, the West and the non-West. Yet, what concerns me here is not so much the arguments themselves as a response they elicited. For, in the discussion that followed, a famous Mexican anthropologist cum international cultural bureaucrat, who had looked increasingly unconvinced through the proceedings, had only one question for the speaker, whom she knew very well. "Have you gone over to the other side, Craig?," she asked with an air of impatient finality.

I was somewhat bewildered at first. But as the conversation continued, I gradually understood what was at stake in the query. The underlying assumption of the anthropologist interlocutor was that alterity and authority have to conform to the analyst's vision of difference and power, tradition and modernity, the non-West and the West, the other and the self. Needless to say, such analytical and extra-analytical assumption was profoundly grounded in entitlement and privilege – affective and experiential – of institutional and everyday academe, alluded to above. Where was the need to query cosmopolitanism, to register different claims on tradition, to recognize distinct visions of modernity? After all, are not such matters (always) explained and (already) set in place through scholarly presumption of the way the world "ought" to be? Here was/is to be found the formidable conceit of pervasive scholasticisms: an immaculate "ought" of the analyst/observer – academic or/and quotidian – that *trumps* over every contentious "is." As the "ought" orchestrates and becomes the "is," those who do not fall in line go over to "the other side."

Untangling Scholasticisms

Scholasticisms entail understandings and orientations that present their particular case as the general story while forgetting the conditions that make this possible: they privilege a view from somewhere as the vista for everywhere; underwrite an adjudicatory rationality as overriding all worldly reasons; universalize ethical and aesthetic judgment by suppressing the social-economic-cultural fields in which such judgments are embedded; and secure their "ought" as riding over each "is" that constitutes the world.[10] Needless to say, all this underlies the pervasive transcendence of modern scholasticisms.

Such scholasticisms and their transcendental claims abound in the academy, as deliberated pieces of scholarship and as routine expressions in its quotidian life, acutely embodying and endorsing, constitutively coining and crafting, entitlement, privilege, and hierarchy – in/as argument, affect, and effect. Indeed, exemplified by the everyday academic encounter that was just recounted, scholasticisms come into play in frontal ways, their arms swinging and their fangs bared, as it were.[11]

All this is easy to establish and undemanding to upbraid. Therefore, I turn now to a more difficult task. Specifically, my bid is to untangle the ways in which the condition of possibility of salient scholarship can consist of its braiding of scholastic persuasions – including, the presence and triumph of the "ought" – with rather more contending dispositions. Such distinct orientations attempt to approach and explicate subjects and worlds in terms of their mundane mix-ups and murkiness, or the contentious "is" that is the stuff of history and politics, words and worlds, and thinking and living. To illustrate this, let me turn – somewhat unconventionally, for a historian-anthropologist who inhabits distinct borderlands – to the work of the European philosopher Jürgen Habermas.

There is method to my madness.

On the one hand, Habermas's (1987) elaborations of reason as "communicative action" and a self-critical modernity have extended the democratic horizons of the "unfinished" Enlightenment project. Thus, when the philosopher posits reason as "communicative action," his protocols of argument at once displace a merely subject-centered rationality and underscore the "counter-discourse" of modernity (Habermas 1984, 1992; McCarthy 1990). They announce immanent issues of an inter-subjective rationality as well an obligation to the other in deliberation.

On the other hand, these tendencies in Habermas's thought are profoundly worked over and consequently marginalized by distinct, overlapping orientations. First, under issue is the imperative in his schemas of the "ought" that is profoundly tied to a scholastic reason. Second, Habermasian projections of an "idealized history" present the past in terms of modular temporal schemes, involving attenuated stages of succession. Third, the philosopher assumes a "telos" that is built into language at large. Lastly, his equation of modernity with Europe, I submit, has an extra-analytical, experiential, and even affective provenance.

Together, my point concerns the requirements of staying with and thinking through these contrasting dimensions yet conjoint dispositions in the thought of Habermas.[12] And I begin appropriately with the philosopher's proposal of the counter-discourse of modernity.

As is generally known, at least to the initiated, Habermas explores the primary crossroads of this counter-discourse to point toward a "path open but not taken: the construal of reason in terms of a non-coercive intersubjectivity of mutual understanding and reciprocal recognition" (McCarthy 1987: xvi). Here are to be found formulations that see reason as ineluctably *situated*, that is to say "as concretized in history, society, body, and language"; view its potential as requiring realization in the "communicative practice of ordinary, everyday life"; and, against totalized critiques of reason, emphasize its capacity to be critical (McCarthy 1987: xvi–xvii).

At the same time, we need to ask if such moves by Habermas (1971, 1984) possibly reduce political power matrices to relations of communication, which "surreptitiously throws the political back onto the terrain of ethics" (Bourdieu 1991, 2000). Likewise, do such measures suppress visceral registers of being and difference to a *telos* of language that provides the model for practical, rational discourse, one that ever tends toward consensus? (White 2000: 36 and 138). Further, what are we to make of feminist critiques that Habermas's understanding of communicative action emphasizes a technical understanding of rationality, which abstracts from as well as delegitimizes particularities of nonlinguistic forms of communicative action (Pajnik 2006a)? Finally, are Habermas's proposals not fused together with his ethnocentric framing of rationality, which itself arguably rests upon his prior, experiential elision of modernity with Europe? Is this what underlies his framing of modernity as an entirely internally self-generated, European phenomenon, occluding any linkages with empire or non-Western worlds?

The point is that to register Habermas's avowal of the situated and critical nature of rationality is to affirm how his thought might be made to address issues of immanence, at least when expressed upon distinct registers of the mundane, the theoretical, and their interplay. Yet, in order to recognize such horizons, the task of careful affirmation must attend to the philosopher's *a priori* presumptions that reveal a transcendent "ought," a formative scholasticism, and an extra-analytical elision of modernity with Europe: these measures circumscribe the exact "is" that his thought avows regarding the situated attributes of rationality. Such simultaneous measures are critical for articulating immanence (yet without turning it into an antidotal, utopian horizon) while tracking scholasticism (but without treating it as a distant, dystopic enemy), since the scholastic and the immanent are ever of the world, which is never innocent.

This brings me to Habermas's (1987: 321–326) emphasis on a community of dialogue. Here, the philosopher endorses how in deliberation the utterance of the other places an obligation on/to the self, while insightfully acknowledging also the unpredictable, potentially disruptive attributes of the utterance in everyday life (White 2000: 37). Indeed, Habermas argues further for the disclosure of particularity that makes it possible for the (now [?] de-centered) subject to "bear witness to the possibility of no-saying" to the identity s/he has projected on the other, despite the subject's investments in the latter's identity (Habermas 1984: 399).

All this is important accomplishment, pointing to the commitment to conversation – as a matter of understanding and living – in contentious worlds formed by heterogeneous subjects, subjects that militate against being indolently contained within safe boundaries of self and other. Approached in this way, Habermas's formulations might even aid our own avowal of immanence. An avowal of immanence rather than the triumph of a transcendental meaning-legislating rationality, one which subjugates all actors, each world, and every other to the sovereign subject's self-same adjudicatory reason. Once again, the possibilities at stake have to be culled from the way that the philosopher's thought inhabits the world – or, is made to do so – as announcing immanence.

Yet, at the very moment of acknowledging such possibilities, let us consider also the other side of Habermas's reasoning on deliberation and dialogue, involving utterance and other. Foremost is the concern that the philosopher's considerations of such issues appear as "typically overshadowed by the excessively precise normative character of the obligation" that Habermas finds the self as incurring (White 2000: 36). This is a move that is itself connected to his belief in eventual consensus (Habermas 1971: 314; 1987: 311). Indeed, Habermas's wider proposals regarding the other and/in argument cannot remain untouched by his "underlying claim that an orientation to consensus is built into the *telos* of language" (White 2000: 36).[13] This leads to the often exclusive, uneasily *a priori*, and unsteadily depoliticizing cast of the philosopher's promulgations on communication and consensus, the inter-subjective and the non-coercive, and language and reason. Scholasticism strikes yet again.

All this has implications, finally, for Habermas's call for a self-critical modernity, whose value in our times of raging authoritarian, governmental, muscular nationalist-populisms we would be churlish to ignore. At the same time, however, the philosophers' proposals are upheld and upbraided by his *a priori* elision of modernity with Europe, such that both these entities-concepts appear as historical fact, theoretical metaphor, and analytical abstraction. Here, it is not only that the West is rehearsed as modernity but that modernity is staged "*as* the West" (Mitchell 2000: 15 emphasis in the original).

At the same time, far from merely pigeonholing Habermas's writing as Eurocentric, such recognition importantly entails entering related protocols of the philosopher's thought. In such procedures, it is not simply an excision of the non-West but rather a patterned, attenuated, idealized history of Europe that itself shores up Habermas's critical theory of modernity. Such idealization marks Habermas's history of the (Western) nation, as ably unraveled by – the self-admittedly "critical Habermasian" – Craig Calhoun (2009: 319–320). They extend to the ways in which Habermas's conception of the liberal public sphere presents an *idealized* history of liberal bourgeois public spheres, refusing to admit to the *plural* traditions of reasoned exchange that marked eighteenth-century Western Europe. Thereby, it ignores how the bourgeois public appropriated and marginalized such more inclusive notions of public participation and discussion by strategically closing off from the arena the range of possible discussants (Calhoun 1992; Bourdieu 2000: 65–66). Particularly poignant here are feminist critiques of how the occlusion of women from the bourgeois public sphere was not a mere accident, but that these public spheres, as recounted by Habermas (and others), were acutely constituted by, premised upon, such gendered exclusions (Fraser 1992; Landes 1993; Pajnik 2006a; see also Goodman 1992; Fleming 1995; Meehan 1995).

Building on these discussions, I would like to suggest that at stake are not mere errors of understanding, analytical and empirical. Rather, such idealized projections of history and society have a deep provenance, wide implications. Consider now Habermas's proposition that under modernity the notion of the "new" or the "modern" world loses a "merely chronological meaning" to take on instead "the oppositional significance of an emphatically 'new' age" (Habermas 1987: 5). This means further that for the philosopher the normative order of modernity has to be ground out of itself, rather than drawing its dispositions from models offered by other, obviously prior, epochs.

Now, as I have argued earlier, on offer is an idealized representation that is at once persuasive and acutely representative (Dube 2017a: 70–73). Indeed, despite their own distinctions, Habermas's formulations are part of wider delineations of modernity that have each entailed a ceaseless interplay between the ideal attributes and the actual manifestations of the phenomenon. This has meant not only that the actual has been apprehended in terms of the ideal, but that even when a gap is recognized between the two the actual (of modernity) is seen as tending toward the ideal (of modernity) with each shoring up the other. Here, it is exactly the admixtures of the actual articulations and the idealized projections of modernity that have defined its worldly dimensions. Taken together, these procedures, announcing hierarchical mappings of time and space, not only order the world but actually constitute it, such that Habermas's propositions participate in the worlding of modernity – as part of an (ultimately) adjudicatory bid to redeem, bring to a close, the unfinished Enlightenment project.[14]

Under discussion are key questions. What is at stake in critically yet carefully entering the protocols of Habermas's thinking? Might such measures reveal the limits of principally lamenting and readily rebutting the absence in "classical" Eurocentric theory of the non-West and empire? Do our assertions and critiques of this kind variously circumscribe critical readings of European thought, its problems and potentialities as betokening each other? Might we trace instead the pervasive subordination of the immanent, the affective, the everyday, the extra-analytical, and the mundane to the imperatives of a scholastic reason, an adjudicatory rationality? Should not such querying be conducted in the widest worlds – non-Western and Western, quotidian and scholarly, and subaltern and elite? Is there not a certain poignancy, pathos even, which is encountered when thinking through scholarly protocols – such as those of Habermas – that attempt to acknowledge and avow difference yet can only do this by returning to a resolutely singular scholastic "ought"? Is it not a matter of foreboding that we are in the face of the legislation of meaning and the ordering of life that remake the world – not only through modular grids but in an exclusive image?

Motif Two

A couple of decades ago, at a workshop on modern historiography in Mexico City, a graduate student raised a question about the necessity of specifying what exactly is at stake in discussing history as always appearing in the image of modernity. The speaker, an upcoming academic star, simply looked away. In the midst of the studied silence, the condescension was palpable. As many of the student's cohort and various certified scholars snickered, even those sympathetic to the query and its spirit looked toward their toes in embarrassment. Here was a public lesson on the unstated requirement to never doubt *doxas*, which beget themselves, as effect and affect of analytical entitlements, everyday hierarchies, and their routine reproduction in academic arenas.

Unable to contain myself, I rephrased the salience of the student's question, emphasizing the need to address at least the coupling of history-writing and the nation under regimes of modernity and their imaginaries. The speaker looked unsettled, yet was about to answer when a very senior historian, a venerable mandarin, seized the microphone. As not only the esteemed chair of the session but the presiding deity of the workshop – and patron of several historians across generations – this don and doyen among scholars, magisterially addressed the audience. To query modernity, nation, and history-writing, he pronounced, was the stuff of new-fangled "postmodern" and "postcolonial" theories. The true historian diligently worked in the archives, far away from such speculation. Yet all that the esteemed historian said about the single-minded purpose of value-free research in the state archives reproduced commonplace assumptions regarding the modern nation and its historiography as the incessant march of progress. Here, the more scholasticism drew sharp boundaries between itself and the mundane as well as the theoretical, the more it tripped itself up in its disorderliness, its complicity with routine statist-developmental imaginaries.

Two weeks later, I was speaking at the weekly colloquia of a distinguished department in a famous university. A little apprehensive, I drew upon my wider construction of an ethnographic history of an "untouchable" community in order to raise issues of the interplay between caste and power, myth and history, and the enchantments of symbols of governance of the modern state and the fabrications of religious legalities by subaltern communities. At the end, I also cast my net somewhat wider. Seizing on ethnographic and historical materials, I spelled out the implications of my analysis for the persistence of routine antinomies – of modernity and tradition, state and community, rationality and ritual, and reason and emotion – within influential strands of social and political theory in western and non-western contexts.

During the discussion, an avant-garde scholar, a bearer of cutting-edge anthropology, put a question to me in the kindest of ways. I was asked about the manner in which my work related to the study of lower-caste and untouchable groups, which the academic stressed was the *real area, the actual field* of my research. In response, I outlined some of the continuities and differences between my work and other studies of Dalit communities. Yet, I also stressed that critical issues of myths and the making of modernity, orality and the construction of histories, and writing and the fashioning of traditions were equally the area(s)/field(s) of my research (Dube 1998). It was a wholly civil exchange. Yet, the to-and-fro has stayed with me in the years after.

At stake was a key distinction, based upon academic entitlement and scholarly hierarchy, between the "is" and an "ought." Here, a study of Dalit, subaltern groups undertaken by a younger historian appeared as an inherent condition of limits for wider theoretical enquiry – the inescapable "is" of academic endeavor. In contrast, a higher status was occupied by the intellectual labor of accomplished analysts, conducting research across multi-sited ethnographic sites, producing theory that was unconstrained by stifling "areas," which is what (we were being told) critical reflection "ought" to be. Scholasticism has many stripes.

Final Sutures

Despite the able efforts of the two distinguished professors (alongside the endeavors of others), I have been unable to give up my habits, which turn on conjunctions of narrative and theory. Around almost two decades ago, articulating everyday legalities/illegalities, colonial cultures, and an evangelical modernity – and issues of meaning, power, and difference, very broadly – I made a case for a "history without warranty" (Dube 2004a). Here are to be found procedures that carefully query "those 'entities' presupposed by our typical ways of seeing and doing in the modern world" (White 2000: 4–5), in order to think through the guarantee of progress under modernity, carefully querying the scandals of the West *and* the nation. To wit, the conceptions, propositions, and outrages queried by a history without warranty intimate not merely objects of knowledge but conditions of knowing, which demand cautious questioning, prudent articulation, and critical affirmation in the wake of careful interrogation (White 2000: 8; Dube 2004a, 2010, 2017a).

I would like to suggest now that my emphases on immanence shift the terms of a history without warranty in a specific manner. Indeed, the explicit acknowledgment and articulation, in work as in life, of the affective and the embodied, the experiential and the extra-analytical, and the quotidian and the mundane – that is to say, of the immanent – as coursing through social worlds has critical consequences. First, despite its avowal of the ontological, the prior somewhat cerebral cast of a history without warranty is now made flesh, blood, and spirit. Moreover, categories (academic and social) are themselves rendered even less as principally instrumental explanatory devices and much more as constitutive attributes of social worlds, which often, variously bear value properties, inviting and inciting meaningful practices. Finally, the earlier emphases of a history without warranty concerning prudent querying and critical affirmation of social worlds now acquire greater immediacy and indeterminacy, interrupted by the uncertain, the uncanny, and the unimaginable. If truth is a matter of wager, a bet that one takes with oneself, as Merleau-Ponty once argued, this is because truth is about life and living, politics and worlds, each betokening the other. These are life-worlds, saturated with immanence, that are ours to carefully question, to ethically articulate, and even to re-enchant amidst the enchantments that abound. This might particularly be the case as we think through entitlement and privilege exactly in order to actively unlearn privilege and entitlement.

Ends

All of this is to ask also if certain key questions simply disappear as we acknowledge the presence of immanence amidst the enchantments of modernity? What is at stake in enquiring whether the most careful, creative of "our" understandings might yet subsume and subordinate – to compelling claims that we hold – contradictory worlds and their contentions? In responding affectively, politically to the urgency of the present are we to abandon the impulse to cautiously probe and critically affirm social worlds with the desire to carefully narrate and searchingly describe them? Taking seriously the requirements of evidence and the fidelity to facts, might we also consider sieving evidence through critical filters while construing facts, times, and spaces unexpected? Can such facts speak in the uneasy echoes of limiting doubt rather than readily deal in satisfying certainties? Is there not something to be learned here regarding anthropology, history, and other enquiries as disciplines of modernity, which contain and unravel their archival tracks?

Notes

1 See especially the section ahead on "Unravelling Immanence."
2 It is such mutual begetting that explains my particular coinage of the term "worldly-scholastic" transcendence, which challenges more familiar associations of transcendence with scholasticism, each as bearing prior meanings, anterior associations that I query. All of this should soon become clearer.

3 Here, as Josef Pieper (2001) has shown, such ready assessments bear closer scrutiny, yet it is important to track as well, following Orlando Bentancor (2017), how scholastic presumption could be implicated in wider projects of power and meaning, such as those of imperial processes and mercantile capitalism.

4 Bert van Roermund (2015) provides a distinct take on "secular transcendence," which intriguingly intersects with aspects of my proposal regarding worldly-scholastic transcendence.

5 Indeed, none of this is to deny the formative plurality, the constitutive not-oneness also of modern subjects who are themselves always equally subjects of modernity (see, for instance, Dube 2017a, 2017b).

6 These are all questions that I have discussed in frontal and fledgling ways elsewhere (Dube 2004a, 2010, 2017a).

7 It should soon become clear that while agreeing with Bilgrami on the "value properties" in the world (including, nature) that make normative demands on us, my arguments equally bear distinct emphases. Thus, Bilgrami assumes that "disenchantment" has been the dominant motif of the modern world over the past four centuries. Against this he posits the creative forces of "enchantment" and its recognition – by the seventeenth-century English radical sects, the Romantics, and Gandhi, for instance – such that power is opposed/undone by difference. Instead, I focus also on how the terms of disenchantment create their own enchantments, which find form and assume substance as antinomies and enticements, categories and contentions, and meanings and practices at the core of social worlds. These come to embody value properties that make claims on subjects and their actions. It only follows that my proposal regarding immanence draws in the affective, the embodied, the experiential, and the extra-analytical as signaling the immanent as a routine part of mundane worlds. Arguably, Bilgrami is not especially concerned with such dimensions of the enchantments of disenchantment and immanence of the everyday.

8 See the discussion in the Introduction.

9 Calhoun's presentation was derived from this text.

10 As already indicated, my debts to Bourdieu (1984, 2000) – alongside my learning from Rancière (1989, 1991, 2004) – are immense here. Given the constraints of space, what I cannot explore are my differences with Bourdieu, especially his frequent formalism and cerebral self-indulgence, which can run counter to my affirmations of the affective, the embodied, and the immanent.

11 Nor is this a matter solely of intellectual arenas: academic modes of argument are appropriated, expropriated, and made anew in wider social terrains.

12 I recognize of course that writings on Habermas and discussions of his work are academic industry. Clearly, my effort is not aimed as either exegesis of or commentary on the philosopher's corpus. Rather, I wish to enter the protocols of his thought and reason(s), albeit on my distinct registers, in order to reveal the contradictory stitches that suture his arguments. Such contradictions and contentions are *not* mere mistakes, but arguably the *conditions of possibility* of his assertions, a matter that I had first approached in Dube (2010). All of this registered, it bears pointing out

that my emphasis on the simultaneous possibilities and problems in the work of Habermas intersects with feminist engagement with his writings. Such engagements underscore at once the democratic horizons suggested and yet the gendered exclusions performed by the following: Habermas's account of the public sphere; his theory of communicative action; his dualistic theory of society; and his discussions of deliberative democracy. Of these, I discuss ahead the first two themes, and shall refer there to feminist criticism on these questions. Here, I would like to acknowledge the astute mapping of this literature by Mojca Pajnik (2006a) in an essay that I have read with some effort in imperfect translation (see also Meehan 1995; Pajnik 2006b).

13 Consider now another statement of Habermas (1984):

> ...the use of language with an orientation to reaching understanding is the *original mode* of language use, upon which indirect understanding, giving something to understand or letting something be understood, and the instrumental use of language in general, are parasitic.
>
> (288 emphasis in the original)

14 I have further discussed such questions in relation to the work of intellectual historians of Europe such as Reinhart Koselleck and Hans Ulrich Gumbrecht in Dube (2010). See also, Dube (2017a).

References

Abbink, J., and J. Salvedra, eds. 2013. *The Anthropology of Elites: Power, Culture and the Complexities of Distinction*. New York: Palgrave Macmillan.

Abrams, P. 1983. *Historical Sociology*. Ithaca, NY: Cornell University Press.

Abu-Lughod, L. 1999. "The Interpretation of Culture(s) after Television." In *The Fate of "Culture": Geertz and Beyond*, edited by S. Ortner. Berkeley: University of California Press, 110–135.

Adelman, J. 2017. "What Is Global History Now?" *Aeon* 2. See: https://aeon.co/essays/is-global-history-still-possible-or-has-it-had-its-moment

Agnani, S. 2013. *Hating Empire Properly: The Two Indies and the Limits of Enlightenment Anticolonialism*. New York: Fordham University Press.

Ahmed, S. 2004. *The Cultural Politics of Emotion*. Edinburgh: Edinburgh University Press.

Alonso, A. M. 1994. "The Politics of Space, Time, and Substance: State Formation, Nationalism, and Ethnicity." *Annual Review of Anthropology* 23: 379–400.

Aloysius, G. 1997. *Nationalism without a Nation in India*. Delhi: Oxford University Press.

Amin, S. 1995. *Event, Metaphor, Memory: Chauri Chaura 1922–1992*. Berkeley: University of California Press.

Amin, S. 2016. *Conquest and Community: The Afterlives of Warrior Saint Ghazi Miyan*. Chicago, IL: University of Chicago Press.

Amin, S., and D. Chakrabarty, eds. 1996. *Subaltern Studies IX: Writings on South Asian History and Society*. Delhi: Oxford University Press.

Anderson, B. 1983. *Imagined Communities: Reflections on the Origin and Spread of Nationalism*. London: Verso.

"Anthropology and Time." 2010. *Annales. Histoire, Sciences Sociales* 65(4): 885–996.

Appadurai, A. 1982. *Worship and Conflict under Colonial Rule: A South Indian Case*. Cambridge: Cambridge University Press.

Arnold, D. 1993. *Colonizing the Body: State Medicine and Epidemic Disease in Nineteenth-Century India*. Berkeley: University of California Press.

Arnold, D., and D. Hardiman, eds. 1994. *Subaltern Studies VIII: Essays in Honour of Ranajit Guha*. New Delhi: Oxford University Press.

Asad, T., ed. 1973. *Anthropology and the Colonial Encounter*. London: Ithaca Press.

Asad, T. 1983. "Anthropological Conceptions of Religion: Reflections on Geertz." *Man* (n.s.) 18: 237–259.

Asad, T. 1993. *Genealogies of Religion: Discipline and Reasons of Power in Christianity and Islam*. Baltimore, MD: Johns Hopkins University Press.

Asad, T. 2003. *Formations of the Secular: Christianity, Islam, Modernity*. Stanford, CA: Stanford University Press.

Asad, T., J. Fernandez, M. Herzfeld, A. Lass, S. C. Rogers, J. Schneider, and K. Verdery. 1997. "Provocations of European Ethnology." *American Anthropologist* 99: 713–730.

Austin-Broos, D. 1997. *Jamaica Genesis: Religion and the Politics of Moral Orders*. Chicago, IL: University of Chicago Press.

Axel, B. K. 2001. *The Nation's Tortured Body: Violence, Representation, and the Formation of a Sikh "Diaspora."* Durham, NC: Duke University Press.

Axel, B. K., ed. 2002a. *From the Margins: Historical Anthropology and Its Futures*. Durham, NC: Duke University Press.

Axel, B. K. 2002b. "Introduction: Historical Anthropology and Its Vicissitudes." In *From the Margins: Historical Anthropology and Its Futures*, edited by B. K. Axel. Durham, NC: Duke University Press, 1–44.

Bailey, F. G. 1957. *Caste and the Economic Frontier: A Village in Highland Orissa*. Manchester: Manchester University Press.

Bailey, F. G. 1969. *Stratagems and Spoils: A Social Anthropology of Politics*. Oxford: Blackwell.

Bama. 2008. *Vanmam: Vendetta*. New Delhi: Oxford University Press.

Banaji, J. 1970. "The Crisis of British Anthropology." *New Left Review* 64: 71–85.

Bandyopadhyay, S. 1997. *Caste, Protest and Identity in Colonial India: The Namasudras of Bengal 1872–1947*. Richmond: Curzon Press.

Banerjee, P. 2006. *Politics of Time: "Primitives" and History-writing in a Colonial Society*. New Delhi: Oxford University Press, 2006.

Banerjee, P. 2011. "Afterword." In *Modern Makeovers: Handbook of Modernity in South Asia*, edited by S. Dube. New Delhi: Oxford University Press, 262–274.

Banerjee, P. 2020. *Elementary Aspects of the Political: Histories from the Global South*. Durham, NC: Duke University Press.

Banerjee-Dube, I. 2007. *Religion, Law and Power: Tales of Time in Eastern India, 1860–2000*. London: Anthem Press.

Banerjee-Dube I. 2015. *A History of Modern India*. Cambridge and New Delhi: Cambridge University Press.

Banerjee-Dube I. and S. Dube. 2009. "Introduction." In *Ancient to Modern: Religion, Power, and Community in India*, edited by I. Banerjee-Dube and S. Dube. New Delhi: Oxford University Press, 1–27.

Barker, J. 2011. *Native Acts: Law, Recognition, and Cultural Authenticity.* Durham, NC: Duke University Press.

Barrera-González, A., M. Heintz, and A. Horolets, eds. 2017. *European Anthropologies.* New York: Berghahn.

Barth, F. 1959. *Political Leadership among Swat Pathans.* London: Athlone Press.

Baucom, I. 2005. *Specters of the Atlantic: Finance Capital, Slavery, and the Philosophy of History.* Durham, NC: Duke University Press.

Bauman Z. 1992. *Intimations of Postmodernity.* London: Routledge.

Bayly, C. A. 1988. *Indian Society and the Making of the British Empire.* Cambridge: Cambridge University Press.

Bear, L. 2007. *Lines of the Nation: Indian Railway Workers, Bureaucracy, and the Intimate Historical Self.* New York: Columbia University Press.

Becker, C. L. 1932. *The Heavenly City of the Eighteenth-Century Philosophers.* New Haven, CT: Yale University Press.

Beckert, S. 2014. *Empire of Cotton: A Global History.* New York: Knopf.

Beckert, S. and C. Desan, eds. 2018. *American Capitalism: New Histories.* New York: Columbia University Press.

Bennett, T. 1995. *The Birth of the Museum: History, Theory, Politics.* London: Routledge.

Bennett, T. 2004. *Pasts beyond Memory: Evolution, Museums, Colonialism.* London: Routledge.

Bentancor, O. 2017. *The Matter of Empire: Metaphysics and Mining in Colonial Peru.* Pittsburgh: University of Pittsburgh Press.

Berlin, I. 2001. *Against the Current: Essays in the History of Ideas.* Princeton, NJ: Princeton University Press.

Berman, R. 2004. *Enlightenment or Empire: Colonial Discourse in German Culture.* Lincoln: University of Nebraska Press.

Bhabha, H., ed. 1990. *Nation and Narration.* London: Routledge.

Bhabha, H. 1994. *Location of Culture.* London: Routledge.

Bhandar, B. 2018. *Colonial Lives of Property: Law, Land, and Racial Regimes of Ownership.* Durham, NC: Duke University Press.

Bhandari, P. 2019. *Money, Culture, and Class: Elite Women as Modern Subjects.* London and New Delhi: Routledge.

Bharti, A., ed. 2013. Special Issue on "Dalit Streevad." *Streekal* 9.

Bhattacharya, N. 2018. *The Great Agrarian Conquest: The Colonial Reshaping of a Rural World.* Ranikhet: Permanent Black.

Bilgrami, A. 2010. "Understanding Disenchantment." See: http://blogs.ssrc.org/tif/2010/09/06/disenchantment/

Bilgrami, A. 2014. *Secularism, Identity, and Enchantment.* Cambridge, MA: Harvard University Press.

Birla, R. 2009. *Stages of Capital: Law, Culture, and Market Governance in Late Colonial India.* Durham, NC: Duke University Press.

Blackburn, R. 2011. *The American Crucible: Slavery, Emancipation and Human Rights.* London: Verso Books.

Bloch, M. 1954. *The Historian's Craft*. Translated by P. Putnam. Manchester: Manchester University Press.

Boas, F. 1928. *Anthropology and Modern Life*. New York: Norton.

Boas, F. 1974. "The History of Anthropology." In *The Shaping of American Anthropology, 1883–1911: A Franz Boas Reader*, edited by G. Stocking, Jr. New York: Basic Books, 23–35.

Bourdieu, P. 1977. *Outline of a Theory of Practice*. Translated by R. Nice. Cambridge: Cambridge University Press.

Bourdieu, P. 1984. *Distinction: A Social Critique of the Judgement of Taste*. Translated by R. Nice. Cambridge, MA: Harvard University Press.

Bourdieu, P. 1991. *Language and Symbolic Power*. Translated by G. Raymond and M. Adamson. Cambridge: Polity Press.

Bourdieu, P. 2000. *Pascalian Meditations*. Translated by R. Nice. Cambridge: Polity Press.

Braudel, F. 1973. *The Mediterranean and the Mediterranean World in the Age of Philip II*. Vols. 1 and 2. Translated by S. Reynolds. London: Fontana/Collins.

Bruno, I. and G. Salle. 2018. "'Before Long There Will Be Nothing but Billionaires': The Power of Elite over the Saint-Tropez Peninsula." *Socio-Economic Review* 16: 435–458.

Burghart, R. 1996. *Conditions of Listening: Essays on Religion, History, and Politics in South Asia*. New Delhi: Oxford University Press.

Burton, A. M. 1998. *At the Heart of the Empire: Indians and the Colonial Encounter in Late-Victorian Britain*. Berkeley: University of California Press.

Butalia, U. 1998. *The Other Side of Silence: Voices from the Partition of India*. New Delhi: Viking Penguin.

Byrne, D. 2014. *Counterheritage: Critical Perspectives on Heritage Conservation in Asia*. New York: Routledge.

Calhoun, C., ed. 1992. *Habermas and the Public Sphere*. Cambridge, MA: MIT Press.

Calhoun, C. 2009. "The Class-Consciousness of Frequent Travelers: Toward a Critique of Actually Existing Cosmopolitanism." In *Enchantments of Modernity: Empire, Nation, Globalization*, edited by S. Dube. London: Routledge, 310–340.

Cannell, F., ed. 2006. *The Anthropology of Christianity*. Durham, NC: Duke University Press.

Cannell, F. 2010. "Anthropology of Secularism." *Annual Review of Anthropology* 39: 85–100.

Carswell, G. 2013. "Dalits and Local Labor Markets in Rural India: Experiences from the Tiruppur Textile Region in Tamil Nadu." *Transactions of the Institute of British Geographers* 38: 325–338.

Chakrabarty, D. 1992. "Postcoloniality and the Artifice of History: Who Speaks for 'Indian' Pasts?" *Representations* 37 (Winter): 1–26.

Chakrabarty, D. 2000. *Provincializing Europe: Postcolonial Thought and Historical Difference*. Princeton, NJ: Princeton University Press.

Chakrabarty, D. 2002. *Habitations of Modernity: Essays in the Wake of Subaltern Studies*. Chicago, IL: University of Chicago Press.

Chakrabarty, D. 2015. *The Calling of History: Sir Jadunath Sarkar and His Empire of Truth*. Chicago, IL: University of Chicago Press.

Chartier, R. 1993. *Cultural History: Between Practices and Representations*. Translated by L. G. Cochrane. Ithaca, NY: Cornell University Press.

Chatterjee, P. 1993. *The Nation and Its Fragments: Colonial and Postcolonial Histories*. Princeton, NJ: Princeton University Press.

Chatterjee, P., and G. Pandey, eds. 1992. *Subaltern Studies VII: Writings on South Asian History and Society*. New Delhi: Oxford University Press.

Chatterjee, P. 2001. *A Time for Tea: Women, Labor, and Post/Colonial Politics on an Indian Plantation*. Durham, NC: Duke University Press.

Chaturvedi, V. 2007. *Peasant Pasts: History and Memory in Western India*. Berkeley: University of California Press.

Clarke, S. 1998. *Dalits and Christianity: Subaltern Religion and Dalit Theology*. New Delhi: Oxford University Press.

Clendinnen, I. 1987. *Ambivalent Conquests: Maya and Spaniard in Yucatán, 1517–1570*. Cambridge: Cambridge University Press.

Clendinnen, I. 1999. *Reading the Holocaust*. Cambridge: Cambridge University Press.

Clifford, J., and G. Marcus, eds. 1986. *Writing Culture: The Poetics and Politics of Ethnography*. Berkeley: University of California Press.

Clough, P. T., and J. Halley, eds. 2007. *The Affective Turn: Theorizing the Social*. Durham, NC: Duke University Press.

Coello de la Rosa, A., and J. M. Dieste, eds. 2020. *In Praise of Historical Anthropology: Perspectives, Methods, and Applications to the Study of Power and Colonialism*. London: Routledge.

Cohen, D. W. 1994. *The Combing of History*. Chicago, IL: University of Chicago Press.

Cohen, D. W., and E. S. A. Odhiambo. 1989. *Siaya: Historical Anthropology*. Cleveland: Ohio University Press.

Cohen, S. 1986. *Historical Culture: On the Recoding of an Academic Discipline*. Berkeley: University of California Press.

Cohn, B. 1980. "History and Anthropology: The State of Play." *Comparative Studies in Society and History* 22: 198–221.

Cohn, B. 1981. "Anthropology and History in the 1980s: Towards a Rapprochement." *Journal of Interdisciplinary History* 12: 227–252.

Cohn, B. 1987. *An Anthropologist among the Historians and Other Essays*. Delhi: Oxford University Press.

Cohn, B. 1996. *Colonialism and Its Forms of Knowledge: The British in India*. Princeton, NJ: Princeton University Press.

Collingham, E. M. 2011. *Imperial Bodies: The Physical Experience of the Raj, c. 1800–1947*. Cambridge: Polity Press.

Comaroff, J. 1985. *Body of Power, Spirit of Resistance: The Culture and History of a South African People*. Chicago, IL: University of Chicago Press.

Comaroff, J. 1989. "Images of Empire, Contests of Conscience: Models of Colonial Domination in South Africa." *American Ethnologist* 16: 661–685.

Comaroff, J., and J. Comaroff. 1986. "Christianity and Colonialism in South Africa." *American Ethnologist* 13: 1–22.

Comaroff, J., and J. Comaroff. 1991. *Of Revelation and Revolution: Christianity, Colonialism, and Consciousness in South Africa*. Vol. 1. Chicago, IL: University of Chicago Press.

Comaroff, J., and J. Comaroff. 1992. *Ethnography and the Historical Imagination*. Boulder, CO: Westview.

Comaroff, J., and J. Comaroff. 1997. *Of Revelation and Revolution: The Dialectics of Modernity on the South African Frontier*. Vol. 2. Chicago, IL: University of Chicago Press.

Comaroff, J., and J. Comaroff. 2009. *Ethnicity, Inc.* Chicago, IL: University of Chicago Press.

Comaroff, J., and S. Roberts. 1981. *Rules and Processes: The Cultural Logic of Dispute in an African Context*. Chicago, IL: University of Chicago Press.

Coombes, A. E. 1994. *Reinventing Africa: Museums, Material Culture, and Popular Imagination in Late Victorian and Edwardian England*. New Haven, CT: Yale University Press.

Cooper, F. 1994. "Conflict and Connection: Rethinking Colonial African History." *American Historical Review* 99: 1519–1526.

Cooper, F. 1996. *Decolonization and African Society: The Labour Question in French and British Africa*. Cambridge: Cambridge University Press.

Corbridge S., J. Harris, and J. Craig, eds. 2013. *India Today: Economy, Politics and Society*. Cambridge: Polity Press.

Coronil, F. 1996. "Beyond Occidentalism: Toward Nonimperial Geohistorical Categories." *Cultural Anthropology* 11: 51–87.

Coronil, F. 1997. *The Magical State: Nature, Money, and Modernity in Venezuela*. Chicago, IL: University of Chicago Press.

Corrigan, P., and D. Sayer. 1985. *The Great Arch: English State Formation as Cultural Revolution*. Oxford: Blackwell.

Cousin, B., and S. Chauvin. 2013. "Islanders, Immigrants, and Millionaires: The Dynamics of Upper-Class Segregation in St Barts, French West Indies." In *Geographies of the Super-Rich*, edited by I. Hay. Cheltenham: Elgar, 186–200.

Cousin, B., S. Khan, and A. Mears. 2018. "Theoretical and Methodological Pathways for Research on Elites." *Socio-Economic Review* 16: 225–249.

Crabtree, J. 2018. *The Billionaire Raj: A Journey through India's New Gilded Age*. New York: OneWorld.

Crapanzano, V. 2000. *Serving the Word: Literalism in America from the Pulpit to the Bench*. New York: New Press.

Curley, R. 2018. *Citizens and Believers: Religion and Politics in Revolutionary Jalisco, 1900–1930*. Albuquerque: University of New Mexico Press.

Daedalus: Journal of the American Academy of Arts and Sciences. 1998. "Special Issue: Early Modernities." 127: v–279.

Daedalus: Journal of the American Academy of Arts and Sciences. 2000. "Special Issue: Multiple Modernities." 129: v–290.

Darnton, R. 1985. *The Great Cat Massacre and Other Episodes in French Cultural History*. New York: Vintage.

Das, V. 1995. *Critical Events: An Anthropological Perspective on Contemporary India*. Delhi: Oxford University Press.

Dasgupta, R. 2014. *Capital: A Portrait of Twenty-First Century*. Delhi. New Delhi: Penguin.

Davin, A. 1978. "Imperialism and Motherhood." *History Workshop* 5: 9–65.

Davis, A., and K. Williams. 2017. "Introduction: Elites and Power after Financialization." *Theory, Culture and Society* 34: 3–26.

Davis, N. 1977. *Society and Culture in Early Modern France: Eight Essays by Natalie Zemon Davis*. Stanford, CA: Stanford University Press.

De Cesari, C. 2010. "Creative Heritage: Palestinian Heritage NGO's and Defiant Arts of Government." *American Anthropologist* 4: 625–637.

Deliège, R. 1992. "Replication and Consensus: Untouchability, Caste and Ideology in India." *Man* (n.s.) 27: 155–173.

Deliège, R. 1997. *The World of the "Untouchables": Paraiyars of Tamil Nadu*. Delhi: Oxford University Press.

Dening, G. 1991. *Mr. Bligh's Bad Language: Passion, Power and Theatre on the Bounty*. Cambridge: Cambridge University Press.

Dening, G. 1995. *The Death of William Gooch: A History's Anthropology*. Honolulu: University of Hawaii Press.

Dening, G. 1996. *Performances*. Melbourne: Melbourne University Press.

Derrida, J. 1996. *Archive Fever: A Freudian Impression*. Translated by E. Prenowitz. Chicago, IL: University of Chicago Press.

Deshpande, P. 2007. *Creative Pasts: Historical Memory and Identity in Western India, 1700–1960*. New York: Columbia University Press.

Di Leonardo, M. 2000. *Exotics at Home: Anthropologies, Others, and American Modernity*. Chicago, IL: University of Chicago Press.

Dirks, N. 1987. *The Hollow Crown: Ethnohistory of an Indian Kingdom*. Cambridge: Cambridge University Press.

Dirks, N. 1989. "The Original Caste: Power, History, and Hierarchy in South Asia." *Contributions to Indian Sociology* 23: 59–77.

Dirks, N. 2002. *Castes of Mind: Colonialism and the Making of Modern India*. Princeton, NJ: Princeton University Press.

Donham, D. 1999. *Marxist Modern: An Ethnographic History of the Ethiopian Revolution*. Berkeley: University of California Press.

Dube, S. 1992. "Myths, Symbols, and Community: Satnampanth of Chhattisgarh." In *Subaltern Studies VII: Writings on South Asian History and Society*, edited by P. Chatterjee and G. Pandey. Delhi: Oxford University Press, 121–158.

Dube, S. 1993. "Idioms of Authority and Engendered Agendas: The Satnami Mahasabha, Chhattisgarh, 1925–50." *The Indian Economic and Social History Review* 30: 383–411.

Dube, S. 1995. "Paternalism and Freedom: The Evangelical Encounter in Colonial Chhattisgarh, Central India." *Modern Asian Studies* 29: 171–201.

Dube, S. 1996a. "Colonial Law and Village Disputes: Two Cases from Chhattisgarh." In *Social Conflict*, edited by N. Jayaram and S. Saberwal. Delhi: Oxford University Press, 423–444.

Dube, S. 1996b. "Telling Tales and Trying Truths: Transgressions, Entitlements and Legalities in Village Disputes, Late Colonial Central India." *Studies in History* 13: 171–201.

Dube, S. 1998. *Untouchable Pasts: Religion, Identity, and Power among a Central Indian Community, 1780–1950.* Albany: State University of New York Press.

Dube, S. 2004a. *Stitches on Time: Colonial Textures and Postcolonial Tangles.* Durham, NC: Duke University Press.

Dube, S. 2004b. "Terms That Bind: Colony, Nation, Modernity." In *Postcolonial Passages: Contemporary History-Writing on India*, edited by S. Dube. New Delhi: Oxford University Press, 1–37.

Dube, S. 2007a. "Anthropology, History, Historical Anthropology: An Introduction." In *Historical Anthropology*, edited by S. Dube. New Delhi: Oxford University Press, 1–73.

Dube, S., ed. 2007b. *Historical Anthropology.* New Delhi: Oxford University Press.

Dube, S., ed. 2009. *Enchantments of Modernity: Empire, Nation, Globalization.* London: Routledge.

Dube, S. 2010. *After Conversion: Cultural Histories of Modern India.* New Delhi: Yoda Press.

Dube, S., ed. 2011. *Modern Makeovers: Handbook of Modernity in South Asia.* New Delhi: Oxford University Press.

Dube, S. 2012. "A Dalit Iconography of an Expressionist Imagination." In *Dalit Art and Visual Imagery*, edited by G. Tartakov. New Delhi: Indian Institute for Dalit Studies and Oxford University Press, 251–267.

Dube, S. 2013a. "Gender aur Satta: Itihas ke Haashiyon par se kuch Samikshatmak Vivaran." In *"Dalit Streevad." Streekal* 9: 35–46.

Dube, S. 2013b. "Unsettling Art: Caste, Gender, and Dalit Expression." *Open Democracy*, posted on 1 August 2013. See: http://www.opendemocracy.net/saurabh-dube/unsettling-art-caste-gender-and-dalit-expression

Dube, S. 2016. "Mirrors of Modernity: Time-Space, the Subaltern, and the Decolonial." *Postcolonial Studies* 19(1): 1–21.

Dube, S. 2017a. *Subjects of Modernity: Time-Space, Disciplines, Margins.* Manchester: Manchester University Press.

Dube, S. 2017b. *Subjects of Modernity, Conversation with Carlos Marichal.* See: https://www.youtube.com/watch?v=2lfYucKbL8Y&feature=emb_logo

Dube, S. 2019a. *El archivo y el campo: Antropología, historia, modernidad.* Ciudad de México: El Colegio de México.

Dube, S. 2019b. "Histories, Dwelling, Habitations: A Cyber-conversation with Dipesh Chakrabarty." In *Dipesh Chakrabarty and the Global South:*

Subaltern Studies, Postcolonial Perspectives, and the Anthropocene, edited by S. Dube, S. Seth, and A. Skaria. London: Routledge, 56–72.

Dube, S. 2020a. "Anthropological Archives: Dalit 'Religions' Redux." *Economic and Political Weekly* LV (34): 42–48.

Dube, S. 2020b. "Historicism and Modernity in the Wake of Provincializing Europe." *Práticas da História – Journal on Theory, Historiography and Uses of the Past* 11: 63–79.

Dube, S. 2021a. "History, Anthropology, and Rethinking Disciplines." In *Oxford Research Encyclopedias: Anthropology*, edited by Mark Aldenerfer. New York: Oxford University Press, 1–40.

Dube, S. 2021b. "Privilegio académico y escolasticismo moderno: Trascendencia secular e inmanencia mundana." *Historia y grafía* 57: 257–290.

Dube, S. 2021c. "Rostros de privilegio: Élites y afectos en Nueva Delhi, India, ca. 1975–2015." *Cuicuilco: Revista de Ciencia Antropológicas* 28(79): 159–182.

Dube, S., and I. Banerjee-Dube, eds. 2019. *Unbecoming Modern: Colonialism, Modernity, Colonial Modernities*. 2nd ed. London: Routledge.

Dube, S., Z. Magubane, and P. Banerjee. n.d. *Decolonize: Three Enquiries in Discipline and Difference*. Manuscript of book under discussion for the Trios Series of the University of Chicago Press.

Dubois, L. 2004. *A Colony of Citizens: Revolution and Slave Emancipation in the French Caribbean, 1787–1804*. Chapel Hill: University of North Carolina Press.

Dubois, L. 2006. "An Enslaved Enlightenment: Rethinking the Intellectual History of the French Atlantic." *Social History* 31: 1–14.

Dumont, L. 1970. *Homo Hierarchicus: The Caste System and Its Implications*. London: The University of Chicago Press.

Eisenstadt, S. N. 1990. "Functionalist Analysis in Anthropology and Sociology: An Interpretive Essay." *Annual Review of Anthropology* 19: 243–260.

Eley, G. 2005. *A Crooked Line: From Cultural History to the History of Society*. Ann Arbor: University of Michigan Press.

Engelke, M. 2007. *A Problem of Presence: Beyond Scripture in an African Church*. Berkeley: University of California Press.

Escobar, A. 2011. *Encountering Development: The Making and Unmaking of the Third World*. Princeton, NJ: Princeton University Press.

Evans-Pritchard, E. E. 1939. "Nuer Time Reckoning." *Africa* 12: 189–216.

Evans-Pritchard, E. E. 1940. *The Nuer: A Description of the Modes of Livelihood and Political Institutions of a Nilotic People*. Oxford: Clarendon Press.

Evans-Pritchard, E. E. 1961. *Anthropology and History*. Manchester: Manchester University Press.

Evans-Pritchard, E. E. 1962. *Social Anthropology and Other Essays*. New York: Free Press of Glencoe.

Evans-Pritchard, E. E. 1965. *Theories of Primitive Religion.* Oxford: Clarendon Press.

Fabian, J. 1983. *Time and the Other: How Anthropology Makes Its Object.* New York: Columbia University Press.

Fabian, J. 1986. *Language and Colonial Power: The Appropriation of Swahili in the Former Belgian Congo.* Cambridge: Cambridge University Press.

Fabian, J. 2000. *Out of Our Minds: Reason and Madness in the Exploration of Central Africa.* Berkeley: University of California Press.

Faubion, J. 1993. "History in Anthropology." *Annual Review of Anthropology* 22: 35–54.

Febvre, L. 1973. *New Kind of History: From the Writings of Febvre.* Translated by K. Folca. London: Routledge.

Ferguson, J. 1990. *The Anti-Politics Machine: Development, Depoliticization, and Bureaucratic Power in Lesotho.* Cambridge: Cambridge University Press.

Ferguson, J. 1999. *Expectations of Modernity: Myths and Meanings of Urban Life on the Zambian Copperbelt.* Berkeley: University of California Press.

Fischer, S. 2004. *Modernity Disavowed: Haiti and the Cultures of Slavery in the Age of Revolution.* Durham, NC: Duke University Press.

Fleming, M. 1995. "Women and the 'Public Use of Reason.'" In *Feminists Read Habermas: Gendering the Subject of Discourse,* edited by J. Meehan. New York: Routledge, 117–137.

Florida, N. 1995. *Writing the Past, Inscribing the Future: History as Prophecy in Colonial Java.* Durham, NC: Duke University Press.

Forman, P. 2012. "On the Historical Forms of Knowledge Production and Curation: Modernity Entailed Disciplinarity, Postmodernity Entails Antidisciplinarity." *Osiris* 27: 156–197.

Foster, R. 1991. "Making National Cultures in the Global Ecumene." *Annual Review of Anthropology* 20: 235–260.

Foucault, M. 1967. *Madness and Civilization: A History of Insanity in the Age of Reason.* London: Tavistock.

Foucault, M. 1970. "The Archeology of Knowledge." *Social Science Information* 9: 175–185.

Foucault, M. 1972. *The Archeology of Knowledge.* Translated by A. M. Sheridan Smith. New York: Pantheon Books.

Foucault, M. 1979. *Discipline and Punish: The Birth of the Prison.* New York: Vintage Books.

Fox, R. 1985. *Lions of the Punjab: Culture in the Making.* Berkeley: University of California Press.

Franklin S. 2007. *Dolly Mixtures: The Remaking of Genealogy.* Durham, NC: Duke University Press.

Fraser, N. 1992. "Rethinking the Public Sphere: A Contribution to the Critique of Actually Existing Democracy." In *Habermas and the Public Sphere,* edited by C. Calhoun. Cambridge, MA: MIT Press, 109–142.

Freeman, J. M. 1979. *Untouchable: An Indian Life History.* Stanford, CA: Stanford University Press.

Fuentes, M. J. 2016. *Dispossessed Lives: Enslaved Women, Violence, and the Archive.* Philadelphia: University of Pennsylvania Press.

Fukuzawa, H. 1991. *The Medieval Deccan: Peasants, Social Systems, and States: Sixteenth to Eighteenth Centuries.* Delhi: Oxford University Press.

Fuller, C. 2004. *The Camphor Flame: Popular Hinduism and Society in India.* Princeton, NJ: Princeton University Press.

Ganti, T. 2014. "Neoliberalism." *Annual Review of Anthropology* 43(1): 89–104.

Geertz, C. 1973. *The Interpretation of Cultures.* New York: Basic Books.

Geertz, C. 1980. *Negara: The Theatre State in Nineteenth Century Bali.* Princeton, NJ: Princeton University Press.

Geismar, H. 2015. "Anthropology and Heritage Regimes." *Annual Review of Anthropology* 44: 71–85.

Genovese, E. 1974. *Roll Jordan Roll: The World the Slaves Made.* New York: Pantheon.

Gerbner, K. 2018. *Christian Slavery: Conversion and Race in the Protestant Atlantic World.* Philadelphia: University of Pennsylvania Press.

Giddens, A. 1979. *Central Problems in Social Theory: Action, Structure, and Contradiction in Social Analysis.* Berkeley: University of California Press.

Gikandi, S. 1996. *Maps of Englishness: Writing Identity in the Culture of Colonialism.* New York: Columbia University Press.

Gilroy, P. 1993. *The Black Atlantic: Modernity and Double-Consciousness.* Cambridge, MA: Harvard University Press.

Ginzburg, C. 1980. *The Cheese and the Worms: The Cosmos of a Sixteenth Century Miller.* Translated by J. Tedeschi and A. Tedeschi. Baltimore: Johns Hopkins University Press.

Ginzburg, C. 1985. *The Night Battles: Witchcraft and Agrarian Cults in the Sixteenth and Seventeenth Centuries.* Translated by J. Tedeschi and A. Tedeschi. New York: Penguin.

Gluckman, M. 1963. *Order and Rebellion in Tribal Africa.* London: Cohen and West.

Goeman, M. 2013. *Mark My Words: Native Women Mapping our Nations.* Minneapolis: University of Minnesota Press.

Gold, A. 2017. *Shiptown: Between Rural and Urban India.* Philadelphia: University of Pennsylvania Press.

Gold, A., and B. R. Gujar. 2002. *In the Time of Trees and Sorrows: Nature, Power, and Memory in Rajasthan.* Durham, NC: Duke University Press.

Goodman, D. 1992. "Public Sphere and Public Life: Toward a Synthesis of Current Historiographical Approaches to the Old Regime." *History and Theory* 32: 1–20.

Goswami, M. 2004. *Producing India: From Colonial Economy to National Space.* Chicago, IL: University of Chicago Press.

Gough, K. 1968. "Anthropology: Child of Imperialism." *Monthly Review* 19: 12–68.

Greenblatt, S. 1991. *Marvelous Possessions: The Wonder of the New World.* Chicago, IL: University of Chicago Press.

Gregory, D. 2007. *The Colonial Present.* Oxford: Blackwell.

Grewal, I. 1996. *Home and Harem: Nation, Gender, Empire, and the Cultures of Travel.* Durham, NC: Duke University Press.

Grosrichard, A. 1998. *The Sultan's Court: European Fantasies of the East.* Translated by L. Heron. London: Verso.

Guasco, M. 2014. *Slaves and Englishmen: Human Bondage in the Early Modern Atlantic World.* Philadelphia: University of Pennsylvania Press.

Guha, R. 1983. *Elementary Aspects of Peasant Insurgency in Colonial India.* Delhi: Oxford University Press.

Guha, R. 1984. "The Prose of Counter-Insurgency." In *Subaltern Studies II: Writings on South Asian History and Society,* edited by R. Guha. Delhi: Oxford University Press, 1–42.

Guha, R. 1997. *Dominance without Hegemony: History and Power in Colonial India.* Cambridge, MA: Harvard University Press.

Guha, R. 2004. "Not at Home in Empire." In *Postcolonial Passages: Contemporary History-Writing on India,* edited by S. Dube. New Delhi: Oxford University Press, 38–46.

Guha, R., ed. 1982–1989. *Subaltern Studies I–VI: Writings on South Asian History and Society.* Delhi: Oxford University Press.

Guha, S. 2014. *Beyond Caste: Identity and Power in South Asia.* Leiden: Brill.

Guha-Thakurta, P., et al. 2014. *Gas Wars: Crony Capitalism and the Ambanis.* New Delhi: Authors UpFront/Paranjoy Guha Thakurta.

Guha-Thakurta, T. 2005. *Monuments, Objects, Histories: Art in Colonial and Post-colonial India.* New York: Columbia University Press.

Gupta, A. 2017. "Changing Forms of Corruption in India." *Modern Asian Studies* 51: 1862–1890.

Gupta, C. 2002. *Sexuality, Obscenity, and Community: Women, Muslims, and the Hindu Public in Colonial India.* Delhi: Permanent Black.

Gupta, C. 2016. *The Gender of Caste: Representing Dalits in Print.* Seattle: University of Washington Press.

Guru, G. 2009. *Humiliation: Claims and Contexts.* New Delhi: Oxford University Press.

Guru, G., and S. Sarukkai. 2012. *The Cracked Mirror: An Indian Debate on Experience and Theory.* New Delhi: Oxford University Press.

Gutiérrez, R. 1991. *When Jesus Came, the Corn Mothers Went Away: Marriage, Sexuality, and Power in New Mexico, 1500–1846.* Stanford, CA: Stanford University Press.

Habermas, J. 1971. *Knowledge and Human Interests.* Translated by. J. Shapiro. Boston, MA: Beacon Press.

Habermas, J. 1984. *The Theory of Communicative Action* 2 vols. Translated by T. McCarthy. Boston, MA: Beacon Press.

Habermas, J. 1987. *The Philosophical Discourse of Modernity: Twelve Lectures.* Translated by F. G. Lawrence. Cambridge, MA: MIT Press.

Habermas, J. 1992. *Postmetaphysical Thinking: Philosophical Essays.* Translated by W. M. Hohengarten. Cambridge, MA: MIT Press.

Hamann, B. E. 2016. "How to Chronologize with a Hammer, Or, The Myth of Homogeneous, Empty Time." *HAU: Journal of Ethnographic Theory* 6: 261–292.

Hamann, B. E. 2020. *Bad Christians, New Spains: Muslims, Catholics, and Native Americans in a Mediterratlantic World.* New York: Routledge.

Hamilton, C., V. Harris, M. Pickover, et al. 2002. *Refiguring the Archive.* Cape Town: David Philip.

Hanks, W. F. 2010. *Converting Words: Maya in the Age of the Cross.* Berkeley: University of California Press.

Hans, R. K. 2016. "Making Sense of Dalit Sikh history." In *Dalit Studies*, edited by R. S. Rawat and K. Satyanarayana. Durham, NC: Duke University Press, 131–154.

Hansen, T. B., and F. Steputtat. 2001. "Introduction: States of Imagination." In *States of Imagination: Ethnographic Explorations of the Postcolonial State*, edited by T. Blom Hansen and F. Stepputat. Durham, NC: Duke University Press, 1–38.

Haraway D. 1990. *Simians, Cyborgs and Women: The Reinvention of Nature.* London: Routledge.

Hardiman, D. 1987. *The Coming of the Devi: Adivasi Assertion in Western India.* Delhi: Oxford University Press.

Harootunian, H. 2002. *Overcome by Modernity: History, Culture, and Community in Interwar Japan.* Princeton, NJ: Princeton University Press.

Hartman, S. H. 1997. *Scenes of Subjection: Terror, Slavery, and Self-Making in Nineteenth-Century America.* New York: Oxford University Press.

Hartman, S. H. 2007. *Lose Your Mother: A Journey along the Atlantic Slave Route.* New York: Farrar, Straus and Giroux.

Hartman, S. H. 2008. "Venus in Two Acts." *Small Axe* 12 (2): 1–14.

Hartog, François. 2009 [1988]. *The Mirror of Herodotus: The Representation of the Other in the Writing of History.* Berkeley: University of California Press.

Hastrup, K., ed. 1992. *Other Histories.* London: Routledge.

Hay, I, ed. 2013. *Geographies of the Super-Rich.* London: Edward Elgar.

Hefner, R. W., ed. 1993. *Conversion to Christianity: Historical and Anthropological Perspectives on a Great Transformation.* Berkeley: University of California Press.

Hefner, R. W. 1998. "Multiple Modernities: Christianity, Islam, and Hinduism in a Globalizing Age." *Annual Review of Anthropology* 27: 83–104.

Henare, A. 2009. *Museums, Anthropology and Imperial Exchange.* Cambridge: Cambridge University Press.

Herzfeld, M. 1982. *Ours Once More: Folklore, Ideology, and the Making of Modern Greece.* Austin: University of Texas Press.

Herzfeld, M. 1985. *Poetics of Manhood: Contest and Identity in a Cretan Mountain Village.* Princeton, NJ: Princeton University Press.

Herzfeld, M. 1987. *Anthropology through the Looking-Glass: Critical Ethnography in the Margins of Europe.* Cambridge: Cambridge University Press.

Herzfeld, M. 1991. *A Place in History: Social and Monumental Time in a Cretan Town*. Princeton, NJ: Princeton University Press.

Herzfeld, M. 1992. *The Social Production of Indifference*. Chicago, IL: University of Chicago Press.

Herzfeld, M. 1997. *Cultural Intimacy: Social Poetics of the Nation-State*. New York: Routledge.

Herzfeld, M. 2009. "The Absent Presence: Discourses of Crypto-colonialism." In *Enchantments of Modernity: Empire, Nation, Globalization*, edited by S. Dube. London: Routledge, 341–371.

Herzfeld, M. 2016. *Siege of the Spirits: Community and Polity in Bangkok*. Chicago, IL: University of Chicago Press.

Herzfeld, M. 2019. "What Is a Polity? 2018 Lewis H. Morgan Lecture." *HAU: Journal of Ethnographic Theory* 9: 23–35.

Hess, L. 2015. *Bodies of Song: Kabir Oral Traditions and Performative Worlds in North India*. New York: Oxford University Press.

Hill, C. 1973. *The World Turned Upside Down: Radical Ideas during the English Revolution*. New York: Penguin Books.

Hill, J., ed. 1988. *Rethinking History and Myth: Indigenous South American Perspectives on the Past*. Chicago, IL: University of Chicago Press.

Hill, R., and T. Myatt. 2010. *The Anti-Economics Textbook: A Critical Thinker's Guide to Micro-Economics*. London: Zed Press.

Ho, K. 2009. *Liquidated: An Ethnography of Wall Street*. Durham, NC: Duke University Press.

Hobsbawm, E. 1993. *Nations and Nationalism since 1780: Programme, Myth, Reality*. Cambridge: Cambridge University Press.

Hyman, L. 2012. *Borrow: The American Way of Debt*. New York: Vintage Books.

Hymes, D., ed. 1972. *Reinventing Anthropology*. New York: Pantheon Books.

Iggers, G. 1995. "Historicism: The History and Meaning of the Term." *Journal of the History of Ideas* 56: 129–152.

Iggers, G. 2012. *The German Conception of History: The National Tradition of Historical Thought from Herder to the Present*. Rev. ed. Middletown, CT: Wesleyan University Press.

Ilaiah. K. 1996. *Why I Am Not a Hindu: A Sudra Critique of Hindutva Philosophy, Culture and Political Economy*. Calcutta: Samya Publications.

Ileto, R. 1979. *Pasyon and Revolution: Popular Movements in the Philippines, 1840–1910*. Manila: Ateneo de Manila University Press.

Jaaware, A. 2018. *Practicing Caste: On Touching and Not Touching*. New York: Fordham University Press.

Jaffrelot, C. 2003. *India's Silent Revolution: The Rise of the Low Castes in North Indian Politics*. New York: Columbia University Press.

Jaffrelot, C. 2005. *Dr. Ambedkar and Untouchability: Fighting the Indian Caste System*. New York: Columbia University Press.

Jangam, Ch. 2017. *Dalits and the Making of Modern India*. New Delhi: Oxford University Press.

Jha, S. 2016. *Reverence, Resistance, and the Politics of Seeing the National Flag*. New Delhi: Cambridge University Press.

Jobson, R. C. 2020. "The Case for Letting Anthropology Burn: Sociocultural Anthropology in 2019." *American Anthropologist* 122: 259–271.

Jodhka, S. S. 2004. "Sikhism and the Caste Question: Dalits and Their Politics in Contemporary Punjab." *Contributions to Indian Sociology* 38: 165–192.

Jodhka, S., and J. Naudet, eds. 2019. *Mapping the Elite: Power, Privilege, and Inequality in Contemporary India*. New Delhi: Oxford University Press.

Juergensmeyer, M. 1982. *Religion as Social Vision: The Movement against Untouchability in 20th-Century Punjab*. Berkeley: University of California Press.

Kaltmeier, O., and M. Rufer, eds. 2017. *Entangled Heritages: Postcolonial Uses of the Past in Latin America*. London: Routledge.

Kapadia, K. 1995. *Siva and Her Sisters: Gender, Caste, and Class in Rural South India*. Boulder, CO: Westview Press.

Kaplan, M. 1995. *Neither Cargo nor Cult: Ritual Politics and the Colonial Imagination in Fiji*. Durham, NC: Duke University Press.

Kasturi, M. 2002. *Embattled Identities: Rajput Lineages and the Colonial State in Nineteenth-Century North India*. New Delhi: Oxford University Press.

Keane, W. 2007. *Christian Moderns: Freedom and Fetish in the Mission Encounter*. Berkeley: University of California Press.

Kelley, D. R. 1998. *Faces of History: Historical Inquiry from Herodotus to Herder*. New Haven, CT: Yale University Press.

Kelly, J. 1991. *A Politics of Virtue: Hinduism, Sexuality, and Countercolonial Discourse in Fiji*. Chicago, IL: University of Chicago Press.

Kelly, J., and M. Kaplan. 1990. "History, Structure, and Ritual." *Annual Review of Anthropology* 19: 119–150.

Kelly, J., and M. Kaplan. 2001. *Represented Communities: Fiji and World Decolonization*. Chicago, IL: University of Chicago Press.

Ketelaar, E. 2001. "Tacit Narratives: The Meanings of Archives." *Archival Science* 1: 131–141.

Khan, S. 2010. *Privilege: The Making of an Adolescent Elite at St. Paul's School*. Princeton, NJ: Princeton University Press.

Khan, S. 2012. "The Sociology of Elites." *Annual Review of Sociology* 38: 361–377.

Khare, R. S. 1984. *The Dalit as Himself: Ideology, Identity, and Pragmatism among the Lucknow Chamars*. New York: Cambridge University Press.

King, T. F. 2019. *The Black Shoals: Offshore Formations of Black and Native Studies*. Durham, NC: Duke University Press.

Klein, K. L. 1999. *Frontiers of Historical Imagination: Narrating the European Conquest of Native America, 1890–1990*. Berkeley: University of California Press.

Knight, D. M. 2015. *History, Time, and Economic Crisis in Central Greece*. New York: Palgrave Macmillan.

Koopman, C. 2010. "Revising Foucault: The History and Critique of Modernity." *Philosophy and Social Criticism* 36: 545–565.

Krause, I. 1988. "Caste and Labor Relations in Northwest Nepal." *Ethnos* 53: 5–36.

Krech III, S. 1991. "The State of Ethnohistory." *Annual Review of Anthropology* 20: 345–375.

Kuper, A. 1973. *Anthropologists and Anthropology: The British School 1922–1972.* London: Allen Lane.

Ladurie, E. L. R. 1979. *Montaillou: The Promised Land of Error.* Translated by B. Bray. New York: Vintage Books.

Lamb, R. 2002. *Rapt in the Name: The Ramnamis, Ramnam, and Untouchable Religion in Central India.* Albany: State University of New York Pres.

Lambek, M. 2002. *The Weight of the Past: Living with History in Mahajanga, Madagascar.* New York: Palgrave Macmillan.

Lambek, M. 2016. "On Being Present to History: Historicity and Brigand Spirits in Madagascar." *HAU: Journal of Ethnographic Theory* 6: 317–341.

Lan, D. 1985. *Guns and Rain: Guerillas and Spirit Mediums in Zimbabwe.* Berkeley: University of California Press.

Landau, P. 1995. *The Realm of the Word: Language, Gender, and Christianity in a Southern African Kingdom.* London: Heinemann.

Landes, J. B. 1993. *Women and the Public Sphere in the Age of the French Revolution.* Ithaca, NY: Cornell University Press.

Larson, P. M. 1997. "'Capacities and Modes of Thinking': Intellectual Engagements and Subaltern Hegemony in the Early History of Malgasy Christianity." *American Historical Review* 102: 968–1002.

Latour, B. 1993. *We Have Never Been Modern.* Translated by C. Porter. Cambridge, MA: Harvard University Press.

Le Goff, J. 1980. *Time, Work, and Culture in the Middle Ages.* Translated by A. Goldhammer. Chicago, IL: University of Chicago Press.

Leach, E. 1954. *Political Systems of Highland Burma: A Study of Kachin Social Structure.* London: G. Bell.

Lee, J. 2018. "Who is the True Halalkhor? Genealogy and Ethics in Dalit Muslim Oral Traditions." *Contributions to Indian Sociology* 52: 1–27.

Levi, G. 1988. *Inheriting Power: The Story of an Exorcist.* Translated by L. Cochrane. Chicago, IL: University of Chicago Press.

Levine, L. 1977. *Black Culture and Consciousness: Afro-American Folk Thought from Slavery to Freedom.* Oxford: Oxford University Press.

Levy, J. 2014. *Freaks of Fortune: The Emerging World of Capital and Risk in America.* Cambridge, MA: Harvard University Press.

Li, D. 2020. *The Universal Enemy: Jihad, Empire, and the Challenge of Solidarity.* Stanford, CA: Stanford University Press.

Lorenzen D. N., ed. 1995. *Bhakti Religion in North India: Community Identity and Political Action.* Albany: State University of New York Press.

Lüdtke, A., ed. 1995. *The History of Everyday Life: Reconstructing Historical Experiences and Ways of Life.* Translated by W. Templer. Princeton, NJ: Princeton University Press.

Lutz, C. A. 1988. *Unnatural Emotions: Everyday Sentiments on a Micronesian Atoll and Their Challenge to Western Theory.* Chicago, IL: University of Chicago Press.

Lutz, C., and J. Collins. 1993. *Reading National Geographic.* Chicago, IL: University of Chicago Press.

Lynch, O.M. 1969. *The Politics of Untouchability: Social Mobility and Social Change in a City of India.* New York: Columbia University Press.

Macdonald, S. 2009. *Difficult Heritage: Negotiating the Nazi Past in Nuremberg and Beyond.* New York: Routledge.

MacKenzie, J. M. 2010. *Museums and Empire: Natural History, Human Cultures, and Colonial Identities.* Manchester: Manchester University Press.

Mahmood, S. 2011. *Politics of Piety: The Islamic Revival and the Feminist Subject.* Princeton, NJ: Princeton University Press.

Makdisi, U. 1997. "Reclaiming the Land of the Bible: Missionaries, Secularism, and Evangelical Modernity." *American Historical Review* 102: 680–713.

Makdisi, U. 2008. *Artillery of Heaven: American Missionaries and the Failed Conversion of the Middle East.* Ithaca. NY: Cornell University Press.

Malinowski, B. 1922. *Argonauts of the Western Pacific: An Account of Native Adventures in the Archipelagoes of Melanesian New Guinea.* London: Routledge.

Malkki, L. 1995. *Purity and Exile: Violence, Memory, and National Cosmology among Hutu Refugees in Tanzania.* Chicago, IL: University of Chicago Press.

Mallon, F. 2005. *Courage Tastes of Blood: The Mapuche Community of Nicolás Ailío and the Chilean State, 1906–2001.* Durham, NC: Duke University Press.

Manderson, L., and M. Jolly, eds. 1997. *Sites of Desire, Economies of Pleasure: Sexualities in Asia and the Pacific.* Chicago, IL: University of Chicago Press.

Mani, L. 1998. *Contentious Traditions: The Debate on Sati in Colonial India.* Berkeley: University of California Press.

Marcus, G. 1997. "The Uses of Complicity in the Changing *mis-en-scène* of Anthropological Fieldwork." *Representations* 59 (Summer): 85–108.

Marcus, G., and D. Cushman. 1982. "Ethnographies as Texts." *Annual Review of Anthropology* 11: 25–69.

Marcus, G., and M. Fischer. 1986. *Anthropology as Cultural Critique: An Experimental Moment in the Human Sciences.* Chicago, IL: University of Chicago Press.

Mathur, S. 2000. "History and Anthropology in South Asia: Rethinking the Archive." *Annual Review of Anthropology* 29: 29–16.

Mathur, S. 2007. *India by Design: Colonial History and Cultural Display.* Berkeley: University of California Press.

Mayaram, S. 1997. *Resisting Regimes: Myth, Memory and the Shaping of a Muslim Identity.* Delhi: Oxford University Press.

Mazzarella, W. 2009. "Affect: What Is It Good For?" In *Enchantments of Modernity: Empire, Nation, Globalization,* edited by S. Dube. London: Routledge, 291–309.

Mazzarella, W. 2017. *The Mana of Mass Society.* Chicago, IL: University of Chicago Press.

Mbembe, A. 2001. *On the Postcolony.* Berkeley: University of California Press.

120 *References*

McCall, J. C. 2000. *Dancing Histories: Heuristic Ethnography with the Ohafia Igbo.* Ann Arbor: University of Michigan Press.

McCarthy, T. 1990. "Introduction." In *Philosophical Discourse of Modernity Twelve Lectures.* Translated by F. G. Lawrence. Cambridge, MA: MIT Press.

McClintock, A. 1995. *Imperial Leather: Race, Gender, and Sexuality in the Colonial Contest.* New York: Routledge.

McCutheon, R. 1997. *Manufacturing Religion: The Discourse on* Sui Generis *Religion and the Politics of Nostalgia.* New York: Oxford University Press.

McDonald, H. 1998. *The Polyester Prince: The Rise of Dhirubhai Ambani.* St. Leonards: Allen and Unwin.

McMahon, D. M. 2002. *Enemies of the Enlightenment: The French Counter-Enlightenment and the Making of Modernity.* New York: Oxford University Press.

Mears, A. 2011. *Pricing Beauty: The Making of a Fashion Model.* Berkeley and Los Angeles: University of California Press.

Medick, H. 1995. "'Missionaries in the Rowboat'? Ethnological Ways of Knowing as a Challenge to Social History." In *The History of Everyday Life: Reconstructing Historical Experiences and Ways of Life,* edited and translated by A. Lüdtke and W. Templer. Princeton, NJ: Princeton University Press, 41–71.

Medick, H., and D. W. Sabean. eds. 1984. *Interest and Emotion: Essays on the Study of Family and Kinship.* Cambridge: Cambridge University Press.

Meehan, J., ed. 1995. *Feminists Read Habermas: Gendering the Subject of Discourse.* New York: Routledge.

Mehta, U. S. 1999. *Liberalism and Empire: A Study in Nineteenth Century British Liberal Thought.* Chicago, IL: University of Chicago Press.

Mencher, J. 1974. "The Caste System Upside Down or the Not-so-mysterious East." *Current Anthropology* 15: 469–493.

Mendelsohn, O., and M. Vicziany. 1998. *The Dalits: Subordination, Poverty and the State in Modern India.* Cambridge: Cambridge University Press.

Menon, R., and K. Bhasin. 1998. *Borders and Boundaries: Women in India's Partition.* New Delhi: Kali for Women.

Merry, S. E. 1992. "Anthropology, Law, and Transnational Processes." *Annual Review of Anthropology* 21: 357–379.

Merry, S. E. 2001. *Colonizing Hawai'i: The Cultural Power of Law.* Princeton, NJ: Princeton University Press.

Meskell, L. 2002. "Negative Heritage and Past Mastering in Archaeology." *Anthropological Quarterly* 75: 557–574.

Meskell, L. 2009. *Cosmopolitan Archaeologies.* Durham, NC: Duke University Press.

Meskell, L. 2012. *The Nature of Heritage: The New South Africa.* Malden, MA: Wiley-Blackwell.

Meskell, L. 2018. *A Future in Ruins: UNESCO, World Heritage, and the Dream of Peace.* New York: Oxford University Press.

Mevani, J. 2022. "Wikipedia Entry on Jignesh Mevani." See: https://en
.wikipedia.org/wiki/Jignesh_Mevani.

Meyer, B. 1999. *Translating the Devil: Religion and Modernity among the Ewe
in Ghana.* Trenton, NJ: Africa World Press.

Meyer, B., and P. Pels, eds. 2003. *Magic and Modernity: Interfaces of Revelation
and Concealment.* Stanford, CA: Stanford University Press.

Middleton, T. 2015. *The Demands of Recognition: State Anthropology and
Ethnopolitics in Darjeeling.* Stanford, CA: Stanford University Press.

Mignolo, W. 1995. *The Darker Side of the Renaissance: Literacy, Territoriality,
and Colonization.* Ann Arbor: University of Michigan Press.

Mihm, S. 2009. *A Nation of Counterfeiters: Capitalists, Con Men, and the
Making of the United States.* Cambridge, MA: Harvard University Press.

Mintz, S. 1960. *Worker in the Cane: A Puerto Rican Life History.* New Haven,
CT: Yale University Press.

Mintz, S. 1985. *Sweetness and Power: The Place of Sugar in Modern History.*
New York: Viking.

Mitchell, T. 1988. *Colonizing Egypt.* Berkeley: University of California Press.

Mitchell, T. 2000. "The Stage of Modernity." In *Questions of Modernity*,
edited by T. Mitchell. Minneapolis: University of Minnesota Press, 1–34.

Mitchell, T. 2002. *Rule of Experts: Egypt, Techno-Politics, Modernity.*
Berkeley: University of California Press.

Mitchell, W. J. T. 2005. *What Do Pictures Want? The Lives and Loves of
Images.* Chicago, IL: University of Chicago Press.

Moffatt, M. 1979. *An Untouchable Community in South India: Structure and
Consensus.* Princeton, NJ: Princeton University Press.

Mohan, S. 2015. *The Modernity of Slavery: Struggles against Caste Inequality
in Colonial Kerala.* New Delhi: Oxford University Press.

Mohanty, C. T. 2003. *Feminism without Borders: Decolonizing Theory,
Practicing Solidarity.* Durham, NC: Duke University Press.

Moore, R. L. 2003. *Touchdown Jesus: The Mixing of Sacred and Secular in
American History.* Louisville, KY: Westminster John Knox Press.

Moreton, B. 2010. *To Serve God and Wal-Mart: The Making of Christian Free
Enterprise.* Cambridge: Harvard University Press.

Morgan, J. 2021. *Reckoning with Slavery: Gender, Kinship, and Capitalism in
the Early Black Atlantic.* Durham, NC: Duke University Press.

Mosse, D. 2012. *The Saint in the Banyan Tree: Christianity and Caste Society
in India.* Berkeley: University of California Press.

Muir, E., and G. Ruggiero, eds. 1991. *Microhistory and the Lost Peoples
of Europe.* Translated by E. Branch. Baltimore, MD: Johns Hopkins
University Press.

Munn, N. 1992. "The Cultural Anthropology of Time: A Critical Essay."
Annual Review of Anthropology: 93–123.

Murphy, E., D. W. Cohen, C. D. Bhimuli, F. Coronil, M. E. Patterson, and
J. Skurski, eds. 2011. *Anthrohistory: Unsettling Knowledge, Questioning
Discipline.* Ann Arbor: University of Michigan Press.

Muthu, S. 2003. *Enlightenment against Empire*. Princeton, NJ: Princeton University Press.

Naepels, M. 2010. "Introduction: Anthropology and History: Through the Disciplinary Looking Glass." *Annales. Histoire, Sciences Sociales* 65(4): 873–884.

Nandy, A. 1995. "History's Forgotten Doubles." *History and Theory* 34: 44–66.

Narayan, B. 2006. *Women Heroes and Dalit Assertion in North India*. New Delhi: Sage Publications.

Narayan, B. 2011. *The Making of the Dalit Public in North India*. New Delhi: Oxford University Press.

Nash, J. 1979. *We Eat the Mines and the Mines Eat Us: Dependency and Exploitation in Bolivian Tin Mines*. New York: Columbia University Press.

Novetzke, C. L. 2016. *The Quotidian Revolution: Vernacularization, Religion, and the Premodern Public Sphere in India*. New York: Columbia University Press.

Ohnuki-Tierney, E. 1987. *The Monkey as Mirror: Symbolic Transformations in Japanese History and Ritual*. Princeton, NJ: Princeton University Press.

Ohnuki-Tierney, E., ed. 1990. *Culture through Time: Anthropological Approaches*. Stanford, CA: Stanford University Press.

Ohnuki-Tierney, E. 1993. *Rice as Self: Japanese Identities through Time*. Princeton, NJ: Princeton University Press.

Ohnuki-Tierney, E. 2002. *Kamikaze, Cherry Blossoms, and Nationalisms: The Militarization of Aesthetics in Japanese History*. Chicago, IL: University of Chicago Press.

Olwig, K. F. 1999. "The Burden of Heritage: Claiming a Place for a West Indian Culture." *American Ethnologist* 26: 370–388.

Omvedt, G. 1994. *Dalits and the Democratic Revolution: Dr. Ambedkar and the Dalit Movement in Colonial India*. New Delhi: Sage Publications India.

Ortner, S. 1984. "Theory in Anthropology since the Sixties." *Comparative Studies in Society and History* 26: 127–132, 135–141.

Ortner, S. 1999. "Introduction." In *The Fate of "Culture": Geertz and Beyond*, edited by S. Ortner. Berkeley: University of California Press, 1–13.

Ortner, S. 2003. *New Jersey Dreaming: Capital, Culture, and the Class of '58*. Durham, NC: Duke University Press.

Ortner, S. 2016. "Dark Anthropology and Its Others: Theory since the Eighties." *HAU: Journal of Ethnographic Theory* 6: 47–73.

Overmyer-Velázquez, M. 2006. *Visions of the Emerald City: Modernity, Tradition, and the Formation of Porfirian Oaxaca, Mexico*. Durham, NC: Duke University Press.

Pajnik, M. 2006a. "Feminist Interpretations of the Public in Habermas's Theory (FEMINISTIČNE INTERPRETACIJE JAVNOSTI V HABERMASOVI TEORIJI)." *Javnost – The Public, Slovene Supplement* 13: 21–36.

Pajnik, M. 2006b. "Feminist Reflections on Habermas's Communicative Action: The Need for an Inclusive Political Theory." *European Journal of Social Theory* 9: 385–404.

Palmié, S., and C. Stewart, eds. 2016. "The Anthropology of History." *HAU: Journal of Ethnographic Theory* 6: 237–369.

Palmié, S., and C. Stewart, eds. 2019. *The Varieties of Historical Experience.* London: Routledge.

Pandey, G. 2001. *Remembering Partition: Violence, Nationalism and History in India.* Cambridge: Cambridge University Press.

Pandey, G. 2006. *Routine Violence: Nations, Fragments, Histories.* Stanford, CA: Stanford University Press.

Pandian, A. 2009. *Crooked Stalks: Cultivating Virtue in South India.* Durham, NC: Duke University Press.

Peel, J. D. Y. 1995. "'For Who Hath Despised the Day of Small Things?' Missionary Narratives and Historical Anthropology." *Comparative Studies in Society and History* 37: 581–607.

Peletz, M. G. 1995. "Kinship Studies in Late Twentieth-century Anthropology." *Annual Review of Anthropology* 24: 343–337.

Pels, P. 1997. "The Anthropology of Colonialism: Culture, History, and the Emergence of Western Governmentality." *Annual Review of Anthropology* 26: 163–183.

Pemberton, J. 1994. *On the Subject of "Java."* Ithaca, NY: Cornell University Press.

Peterson, D. 1999. "Translating the Word: Dialogism and Debate in Two Gikuyu Dictionaries." *Journal of Religious History* 23: 31–50.

Pieper, J. 2001. *Scholasticism: Personalities and Problems of Medieval Philosophy.* South Bend, IN: St. Augustine's Press.

Pinney, C. 1997. *Camera Indica: The Social Life of Indian Photographs.* Chicago, IL: University of Chicago Press.

Pinney, C. 2004. *Photos of the Gods: The Printed Image and Political Struggle in India.* London: Reaktion Books.

Pocock, J. G. A. 1999. *Barbarism and Religion: Volume Two, Narratives of Civil Government.* Cambridge: Cambridge University Press.

Polanyi, K. 1944. *The Great Transformation: The Political and Economic Origin of Our Time.* New York: Farrar and Rinehart.

Poole, D. 1997. *Vision, Race, and Modernity: A Visual Economy of the Andean Image World.* Princeton, NJ: Princeton University Press.

Pooley, W. 2018. "Native to the Past: History, Anthropology, and Folklore." *Past and Present* 239: e1–e15.

Porter, R. 2000. *Enlightenment: Britain and the Creation of the Modern World.* London: Allen Lane.

Porter, R. 2001. *The Creation of the Modern World: The Untold Story of the British Enlightenment.* New York: Norton.

Povinelli, E. A. 2002. *The Cunning of Recognition: Indigenous Alterities and the Making of Australian Multiculturalism.* Durham, NC: Duke University Press.

Povinelli, E. A. 2016. *Geontologies: A Requiem to Late Liberalism.* Durham, NC: Duke University Press.

Prakash, G. 1990. *Bonded Histories: Genealogies of Labor Servitude in Colonial India.* Cambridge: Cambridge University Press.

Prakash, G. 1994. "Subaltern Studies as Postcolonial Criticism." *American Historical Review* 99: 1475–1494.

Prasad, Ch. Bh. 2006. *Dalit Phobia: Why do They Hate Us?* New Delhi: Vitasta Publishing Private Limited.

Prashad, V. 2000. *Dalit Freedom: A Social History of a Dalit Community.* New Delhi: Oxford University Press.

Pratt, M. L. 1992. *Imperial Eyes: Travel Writing and Transculturation.* London: Routledge.

Price, R. 1983. *First-Time: The Historical Vision of an Afro-American People.* Baltimore, MD: Johns Hopkins University Press.

Price, R. 1990. *Alabi's World.* Baltimore, MD: Johns Hopkins University Press.

Price, R. 1998. *The Convict and the Colonel: A Story of Colonialism and Resistance in the Caribbean.* Boston, MA: Beacon Press.

Quigley, D. 1993. *The Interpretation of Caste.* Oxford: Oxford University Press.

Rabasa, J. 2000. *Writing Violence on the Northern Frontier: The Historiography of Sixteenth-Century New Mexico and Florida and the Legacy of Conquest.* Durham, NC: Duke University Press.

Rabasa, J. 2011. *Tell Me the Story of How I Conquered You: Elsewheres and Ethnosuicide in the Colonial Mesoamerican World.* Austin: University of Texas Press.

Rabinow, P. 1989. *French Modern: Norms and Forms of the Social Environment.* Cambridge, MA: MIT Press.

Radcliffe-Brown, A. R. 1952. *Structure and Function in Primitive Society.* Glencoe, IL: Free Press.

Rafael, V. 1988. *Contracting Colonialism: Translation and Christian Conversion in Tagalog Society under Early Spanish Rule.* Ithaca, NY: Cornell University Press.

Raheja, G. G. 1988. *The Poison in the Gift: Ritual, Prestation, and the Dominant Caste in a North Indian Village.* Chicago, IL: University of Chicago Press.

Rajagopal, A. 2011. "The Emergency as Prehistory of the New Indian Middle Class." *Modern Asian Studies* 45(5): 1003–1049.

Rajchman, J. 2001. "Introduction." In *Pure Immanence: Essays on a Life*, by G. Deleuze. New York: Zone, 7–23.

Rancière, J. 1989. *The Nights of Labor: The Workers' Dream in Nineteenth-Century France.* Translated by J. Drury. Philadelphia, PA: Temple University Press.

Rancière, J. 1991. *The Ignorant Schoolmaster: Five Lessons in Intellectual Emancipation.* Translated by K. Ross. Stanford, CA: Stanford University Press.

Rancière, J. 1994. *The Names of History: On the Poetics of Knowledge.* Translated by H. Melehy. Minneapolis: University of Minnesota Press.

Rancière, J. 2004. *The Philosopher and His Poor.* Translated by A. Parker, C. Oster, and J. Drury. Durham, NC: Duke University Press.

Rao, A. 2009. *The Caste Question: Dalits and the Politics of Modern India.* Berkeley: University of California Press.

Rappaport, J. 1994. *Cumbe Reborn: An Andean Ethnography of History.* Chicago, IL: University of Chicago Press.

Rappaport, J. 2005. *Intercultural Utopias: Public Intellectuals, Cultural Experimentation, and Ethnic Pluralism in Colombia.* Durham, NC: Duke University Press.

Rawat, R. S. 2011. *Reconsidering Untouchability: Chamars and Dalit History in North India.* Bloomington: University of Indiana Press.

Rawat, R. S. 2015. "Genealogies of the Dalit Political: The Transformation of Achhut from 'Untouched' to 'Untouchable' in Early Twentieth-century North India." *The Indian Economic and Social History Review* 52: 335–355.

Rawat, R. S., and K. Satyanarayana, eds. 2016. *Dalit Studies.* Durham, NC: Duke University Press.

Rebel, H. 1989. "Cultural Hegemony and Class Experience: A Critical Reading of Recent Ethnological-historical Approaches (Parts One and Two)." *American Ethnologist* 16: 117–136, 350–365.

Reddy, W. 1999. "Emotional Liberty: Politics and History in the Anthropology of Emotions." *Cultural Anthropology* 14: 256–288.

Redfield, P. 2000. *Space in the Tropics: From Convicts to Rockets in French Guiana.* Berkeley: University of California Press.

Redfield, R. 1956. *Peasant, Society, and Culture.* Chicago, IL: University of Chicago Press.

Rege, Sh. 2006. *Writing Caste, Writing Gender: Narrating Dalit Women's Testimonies.* New Delhi: Zubaan Books.

Robbins, J. 2004. *Becoming Sinners: Christianity and Moral Torment in a Papua New Guinea Society.* Berkeley: University of California Press.

Roberts, N. 2016. *To Be Cared For: The Power of Conversion and Foreignness of Belonging in an Indian Slum.* Berkeley: University of California Press.

Rosaldo, R. 1980. *Ilongot Headhunting 1883–1974: A Study in Society and History.* Stanford, CA: Stanford University Press.

Rose Hunt, N. 1999. *A Colonial Lexicon of Birth Ritual, Medicalization, and Mobility in the Congo.* Durham, NC: Duke University Press.

Roseberry, W. 1989. *Anthropologies and Histories: Essays in Culture, History, and Political Economy.* New Brunswick, NJ: Rutgers University Press.

Roy, A. 2005. *Gendered Citizenship: Historical and Conceptual Explorations.* Hyderabad: Orient Longman.

Rufer, M. 2010. *La nación en escenas: Memoria pública y usos del pasado en contextos poscoloniales.* CDMX: El Colegio de México.

Sabean, D. W. 1984. *Power in the Blood: Popular Culture and Village Discourse in Early Modern Germany.* Cambridge: Cambridge University Press.

Sabean, D. W. 1990. *Property, Production and Family in Neckarhausen, 1700–1870.* Cambridge: Cambridge University Press.

Sabean, D. W. 1998. *Kinship in Neckarhausen, 1700–1870.* Cambridge: Cambridge University Press.

Sahlins, M. 1985. *Islands of History*. Chicago, IL: University of Chicago Press.

Sahlins, M. 1993. "Goodbye to *Tristes Tropes*: Ethnography in the Context of Modern World History." *Journal of Modern History* 65: 1–25.

Said, E. W. 1978. *Orientalism*. New York: Pantheon.

Said, E. W. 1995. *Culture and Imperialism*. New York: Vintage.

Saldaña-Portillo, M. 2003. *The Revolutionary Imagination in the Americas and the Age of Development*. Durham, NC: Duke University Press.

Saldaña-Portillo, M. 2016. *Indian Given: Racial Geographies across Mexico and the United States*. Durham, NC: Duke University Press.

Saler, M. 2012. *As If: Modern Enchantment and the Literary Prehistory of Virtual Reality*. New York: Oxford University Press.

Sarkar, S. 1997. *Writing Social History*. Delhi: Oxford University Press.

Sarkar, T. 2001. *Hindu Wife, Hindu Nation: Community, Religion, and Cultural Nationalism*. Delhi: Permanent Black.

Schapera, I. 1962. "Should Anthropologists Be Historians?" *Man* 93: 198–222.

Schmitt, J.C. 1983. *The Holy Greyhound: Guinefort, Healer of Children since the Thirteenth Century*. Translated by M. Thorn. Cambridge: Cambridge University Press.

Schmitt, J.C. 1998. *Ghosts in the Middle Ages: The Living and the Dead in Medieval Society*. Translated by F. T. Lavender. Chicago, IL: University of Chicago Press.

Schmitt, J.C. 2012. *The Conversion of Herman the Jew: Autobiography, History, and Fiction in the Twelfth Century*. Translated by A. J. Novikoff. Philadelphia: University of Pennsylvania Press.

Scott, D. 1994. *Formations of Ritual: Colonial and Anthropological Discourses on the Sinhala Yaktovil*. Minneapolis: University of Minnesota Press.

Scott, D. 2005. *Conscripts of Modernity: The Tragedy of Colonial Enlightenment*. Durham, NC: Duke University Press.

Scott, J. W. 1988. *Gender and the Politics of History*. New York: Columbia University Press.

Scott, J. W. 1996. *Only Paradoxes to Offer: French Feminists and the Rights of Man*. Cambridge, MA: Harvard University Press.

Scott, R. 2005. *Degrees of Freedom: Louisiana and Cuba after Slavery*. Cambridge, MA: Harvard University Press.

Sen, D. 2018. *The Decline of the Caste Question: Jogendranath Mandal and the Defeat of Dalit Politics in Bengal*. Cambridge: Cambridge University Press.

Seth, S. 2007. *Subject Lessons: The Western Education of Colonial India*. Durham, NC: Duke University Press.

Sewell, W., Jr. 1980. *Work and Revolution in France: The Language of Labor from the Old Regime to 1848*. New York: Cambridge University Press.

Sewell, W., Jr. 2005. *Logics of History: Social Theory and Social Transformation*. Chicago, IL: University of Chicago Press.

Shankaran, K. 2021. "On the Pitfalls of Geo-Cultural Pluralism in IR." *International Political Review* 9: 276–279.

Sherinian, Z. C. 2014. *Tamil Folk Music as Dalit Liberation Theology.* Bloomington: Indiana University Press.

Sherman, R. 2007. *Class Acts: Service and Inequality in Luxury Hotels.* Berkeley: University of California Press.

Sherman, R. 2017. *Uneasy Street: The Anxieties of Affluence.* Princeton, NJ: Princeton University Press.

Shilliam, R. 2021. *Decolonizing Politics: An Introduction.* Cambridge: Polity Press.

Shore, C., and S. Nugent, eds. 2002. *Elite Cultures: Anthropological Perspectives.* London and New York: Routledge.

Shyrock, A. 1997. *Nationalism and the Genealogical Imagination: Oral History and Textual Authority in Tribal Jordan.* Berkeley: University of California Press.

Sider, G. 1980. "The Ties that Bind: Culture and Agriculture, Property and Propriety in the New Foundland Village Fishery." *Social History* 5: 1–39.

Sider, G. 1986. *Culture and Class: A Newfoundland Illustration.* Cambridge: Cambridge University Press.

Simpson, A. 2014. *Mohawk Interruptus: Political Life across the Borders of States.* Durham, NC: Duke University Press.

Simpson, A. 2020. "The Sovereignty of Critique." *South Atlantic Quarterly* 119(4): 685–699.

Simpson, A., and A. Smith, eds. 2014. *Theorizing Native Studies.* Durham, NC: Duke University Press.

Sinha, M. 1995. *Colonial Masculinity: The "Manly Englishman" and the "Effeminate Bengali" in the Late Nineteenth Century.* Manchester: Manchester University Press.

Sinha, M. 2006. *Spectres of Mother India: The Global Restructuring of an Empire.* Durham, NC: Duke University Press.

Sivaramakrishnan, K. 1999. *Modern Forests: Statemaking and Environmental Change in Colonial Eastern India.* New Delhi: Oxford University Press.

Skaria, A. 1999. *Hybrid Histories: Forest, Frontiers and Wildness in Western India.* New Delhi: Oxford University Press.

Sklansky, J. 2012. "The Elusive Sovereign: New Intellectual and Social Histories of Capitalism." *Modern Intellectual History* 9: 233–248.

Stewart, C. 2017. *Dreaming and Historical Consciousness in Island Greece.* Chicago, IL: University of Chicago Press.

Stewart, K. 2007. *Ordinary Affects.* Durham, NC: Duke University Press.

Stocking, G., Jr. 1987. *Victorian Anthropology.* New York: Free Press.

Stocking, G., Jr. 1992. *The Ethnographer's Magic and Other Essays in the History of Anthropology.* Madison: University of Wisconsin Press.

Stocking, G., Jr. 1995. *After Tylor: British Social Anthropology 1888–1951.* Madison: University of Wisconsin Press.

Stoler, A. L. 1985. *Capitalism and Confrontation in Sumatra's Plantation Belt.* New Haven, CT: Yale University Press.

Stoler, A. L. 1989. "Rethinking Colonial Categories: European Communities and the Boundaries of Rule." *Comparative Studies in Society and History* 13: 134–161.

Stoler, A. L. 1995a. *Race and the Education of Desire: Foucault's* History of Sexuality *and the Colonial Order of Things*. Durham, NC: Duke University Press.

Stoler, A. L. 1995b. "(P)refacing Capitalism and Confrontation in 1995." In *Capitalism and Confrontation in Sumatra's Plantation Belt*, 2nd ed., by A. Stoler. Ann Arbor: University of Michigan Press, vii–xxxiv.

Stoler, A. L. 2002. *Carnal Knowledge and Imperial Power: Race and the Intimate in Colonial Rule*. Berkeley: University of California Press.

Stoler, A. L. 2008. *Along the Archival Grain: Epistemic Anxieties and Colonial Common Sense*. Princeton, NJ: Princeton University Press.

Stoler, A. L., and F. Cooper. 1997. "Between Metropole and Colony: Rethinking a Research Agenda." In *Tensions of Empire: Colonial Cultures in a Bourgeois World*, edited by F. Cooper and A. L. Stoler. Berkeley: University of California Press, 1–56.

Subramanian, A. 2009. *Shorelines: Spaces and Rights in South Asia*. Stanford, CA: Stanford University Press.

Sunder Rajan, R. 2003. *Scandal of the State: Women, Law, and Citizenship in Postcolonial India*. Durham, NC: Duke University Press.

Tarlo, E. 1996. *Clothing Matters: Dress and Identity in India*. Chicago, IL: University of Chicago Press.

Tarlo, E. 2003. *Unsettling Memories: Narratives of India's "Emergency."* Delhi: Permanent Black.

Taussig, M. 1980. *The Devil and Commodity Fetishism in South America*. Chapel Hill: University of North Carolina Press.

Taussig, M. 1985. *Shamanism, Colonialism, and the Wild Man: A Study in Terror and Healing*. Chicago, IL: University of Chicago Press.

Taussig, M. 1997. *The Magic of the State*. New York: Routledge.

Taussig, M. 2004. *My Cocaine Museum*. Chicago, IL: University of Chicago Press.

Tellmann, U. 2017. *Life and Money: The Genealogy of Liberal Economy and the Displacement of Politics*. New York: Columbia University Press.

Teltumbde, A. 2017. *Dalits: Past, Present, and Future*. New Delhi: Routledge.

Teltumbde, A., and S. Yengde, eds. 2018. *The Radical in Ambedkar: Critical Reflections*. New Delhi: Penguin Random House.

Thapar, R. 2002. Śakuntala: Texts, Readings, Histories. London: Anthem.

Thapar, R. 2005. *Somanatha: The Many Voices of History*. London: Verso.

Thomas, K. 1963. "History and Anthropology." *Past and Present* 24: 3–24.

Thomas, K. 1971. *Religion and the Decline of Magic: Studies in Popular Beliefs in Sixteenth- and Seventeenth-Century England*. London: Weidenfeld and Nicolson.

Thomas, N. 1989. *Out of Time: History and Evolution in Anthropological Discourse*. Cambridge: Cambridge University Press.

Thomas, N. 1991. *Entangled Objects: Exchange, Material Culture, and Colonialism in the Pacific*. Cambridge, MA: Harvard University Press.

Thomas, N. 1994. *Colonialism's Culture: Anthropology, Travel and Government*. Princeton, NJ: Princeton University Press.

Thomas, N. 1997. *In Oceania: Visions, Artifacts, Histories*. Durham, NC: Duke University Press.

Thompson, E. P. 1972. "Anthropology and the Discipline of Historical Context." *Midland History* 1: 45–53.

Thompson, E. P. 1977. "Folklore, Anthropology, and Social History." *Indian Historical Review* 3: 247–266.

Thompson, E. P. 1978. *The Poverty of Theory and Other Essays*. New York: Monthly Review Press.

Thompson, E. P. 1993. *Customs in Common: Studies in Traditional Popular Culture*. New York: New Press.

Thorat, S. 2009. *Dalits in India: Search for a Common Destiny*. New Delhi: Sage.

Thurner, M. 2011. *History's Peru: The Poetics of Colonial and Postcolonial Historiography*. Gainesville: University Press of Florida.

Trouillot, M.R. 1991. "Anthropology and the Savage Slot: The Poetics and Politics of the Otherness." In *Recapturing Anthropology: Working in the Present*, edited by R. Fox. Santa Fe: School of American Research Press, 17–44.

Trouillot, M.R. 1995. *Silencing the Past: Power and the Production of History*. Boston, MA: Beacon Press.

Trouillot, M.R. 2010. "North Atlantic Universals: Analytical Fictions 1492–1945." In *Enchantments of Modernity: Empire, Nation, Globalization*, edited by S. Dube. London: Routledge, 45–66.

Turner, V. 1957. *Schism and Continuity in an African Society*. Manchester: Manchester University Press.

Uberoi, J. P. S. 1962. *The Politics of the Kula Ring: An Analysis of the Findings of Bronislaw Malinowski*. Manchester: Manchester University Press.

van der Veer, P. 1994. *Religious Nationalism: Hindus and Muslims in India*. Berkeley: University of California Press.

van der Veer, P. 2001. *Imperial Encounters: Religion and Modernity in India and Britain*. Princeton, NJ: Princeton University Press.

van Roermund, B. 2015. "Kelsen, Secular Religion, and the Problem of Transcendence." *Netherlands Journal of Legal Philosophy* 44: 100–115.

Vansina, J. 1985. *Oral Tradition as History*. Madison: University of Wisconsin Press.

Vaughan, M. 1991. *Curing Their Ills: Colonial Power and African Illness*. Stanford, CA: Stanford University Press.

Viazzo, P. P. 2003. *Introducción a la antropología histórica*. Lima: Pontificia Universidad Católica del Perú and Instituto Italiano de Cultura.

Vincent, J. 1990. *Anthropology and Politics: Visions, Traditions, and Trends*. Tucson: University of Arizona Press.

Viramma, J. Racine, and J. L. Racine. 1997. *Viramma: Life of an Untouchable.* London: Verso.

Viswanath, R. 2014. *The Pariah Problem: Caste, Religion, and the Social in Modern India.* New York: Columbia University Press.

Voekel, P. 2002. *Alone before God: The Religious Origins of Modernity in Mexico.* Durham, NC: Duke University Press.

Waghmore, S. 2013. *Civility against Caste: Dalit Politics and Citizenship in Western India.* New Delhi: Sage Publications.

Wallerstein, I., ed. 1996. *Open the Social Science: Report of the Gulbenkian Commission on the Restructuring of the Social Sciences.* Stanford, CA: Stanford University Press.

Weidman, A. J. 2006. *Singing the Classical, Voicing the Modern: The Postcolonial Politics of Music in South India.* Durham, NC: Duke University Press.

White, H. 1994. "Foreword: Rancière's Revisionism." In *The Names of History: On the Poetics of Knowledge,* by J. Rancière, edited and translated by H. Melehy. Minneapolis: University of Minnesota Press, vii–xx.

White, L. 2000. *Speaking with Vampires: Rumor and History in Colonial Africa.* Berkeley: University of California Press.

White, S. K. 2000. *Sustaining Affirmation: The Strengths of Weak Ontology in Political Theory.* Princeton, NJ: Princeton University Press.

Williams, R. 1973. "Base and Superstructure in Marxist Cultural Analysis." *New Left Review* 82: 3–16.

Winter, T. 2014. "Heritage Studies and the Privileging of Theory." *International Journal of Heritage Studies* 20: 1–17.

Wolf, E. 1959. *Sons of the Shaking Earth.* Chicago, IL: University of Chicago Press.

Wolf, E. 1982. *Europe and the People without History.* Berkeley: University of California Press.

Wolfe, P. 1997. "History and Imperialism: A Century of Theory, from Marx to Postcolonialism." *American Historical Review* 102: 380–420.

Wolfe, P. 1999. *Settler Colonialism and the Transformation of Anthropology: The Politics and Poetics of an Ethnographic Event.* London: Cassell.

Worsley, P. 1957. *The Trumpet Shall Sound: A Study of "Cargo" Cults in Melanesia.* London: MacGibbon and Keo.

Wright, M. n.d. "A World without Most of Us: Achille Mbembe's *Critique of Black Reason* and the Politics of the Postcolonial Critique." Unpublished manuscript.

Yengde, S. 2019. *Caste Matters.* New Delhi: Penguin Random House.

Zammito, J. 2002. *Kant, Herder, and the Birth of Anthropology.* Chicago, IL: University of Chicago Press.

Index

Note: Page numbers followed by "n" denote endnotes.

Adivasi 16n5, 56, 63n28
aesthetics xi, 59, 92
affect 1, 2, 5, 12, 14, 16n6, 73, 91,
  93, 100; *see also* embodiment;
  entitlement; immanence
Africa ix, x, 2, 9, 28
agency 27, 71
agriculture 67, 68
Alltagsgeschichte ("history of
  everyday life") 33
Alosyius, G. 46
alterity xi, 3–4, 8, 10, 11, 13, 16n3,
  18n14, 20, 31–38 *passim*, 45–48
  passim, 65, 72, 73, 88, 92, 94,
  97, 99
Ambedkar, B. R. 48, 61n12, 62n21
ambivalence 4, 20, 44n19
America 6, 31–33, 66, 91; *see also*
  Latin America
analytical 6–15 *passim*, 19–22 *passim*,
  25–28 *passim*, 31, 38, 46–49 *passim*,
  66, 83n3, 86, 88, 91, 92, 96, 98
Anderson, Benedict 37, 44n20
Annales School, the 27, 32, 43n13,
  43n14
Anthropocene 15
anthropology 5, 47, 49, 52, 54, 60n10,
  63–64 n23, 72–73, 92, 93, 98; *see*
  also discipline
anticolonial 29, 32, 38
anti-essentialism 3
anti-modernist ix, x, 91
antinomies 4, 6–9, 16n3, 18n14,
  20–21, 25–27, 30, 33, 41, 42n3, 50,

54, 59n3, 69, 86, 90, 98, 101n7; *see*
  also discipline
archives 2, 6–8, 11–15 *passim*, 16n3,
  24, 33, 35, 39, 45, 49, 51, 52, 55, 59,
  62n18, 65, 66, 87, 98
Asad, Talal 8, 29, 31, 40, 45
Asia 2, 9
authority *see* alterity; Dalit
autonomy 10, 18n14, 28, 43n13,
  43n15, 50, 58
Axel, Brian 42n2

Bahujan 46–48, 59, 61n12
Bahujan Samaj Party (BSP) 63n24
Bama 46
Banerjee, Prathama 16n5
Banerjee-Dube, Ishita 61n11, 62n18,
  63n26
Basavanna 48
Bayly, C. A. 62n18
Benjamin, Walter 83
Bentancor, Orlando 101n3
Bhabha, Homi 37, 44n19
Bhattacharya, Neeladri 62n18
biblical 21–23, 42n7
Bilgrami, Akil 89–90, 101n7
Boas, Franz 23–24, 25, 42n8
Bourdieu, Pierre 87, 94, 96, 101n10
Brahman 50–52, 55–57 *passim*, 60n9,
  61n11, 62n23
Braudel, Fernand 43n14
Britain 21
British Communist Group of
  Historians 32

Calhoun, Craig 91–92, 96, 101n9
capital *see* capitalism
capitalism x, 1, 4, 6, 10, 13–14, 16n5,
    18n12, 29–32 *passim*, 34, 65–85
    passim, 101n3
caste 15n1, 16n5, 66, 72, 74, 77, 82,
    84n11, 89, 98; *see also* Dalit
Chakrabarty, Dipesh 25, 37
Chatterjee, Partha 38
Chhattisgarh 47, 54, 61n11, 62n18
Chokha Mela 48
Christianity 40, 50, 52, 61n11, 62n21,
    63–64n28
citizen xi, 37, 38, 69, 92
citizenship *see* citizen
civilization 11, 21–25, 28, 42n5,
    43n14
civilized 6–8, 13, 21, 23, 27, 36, 41, 53
class 58, 65, 67, 69, 75, 76, 77, 79,
    89; *see also* middle-class; working-
    class; elite
class of 1979 *see* cohort
coeval 5, 26
coevalness *see* coeval
Cohn, Bernard S. 30, 34
cohort 1, 14, 65–66, 69–78 *passim*,
    80–82, 83n2, 84nn7–8, 97
Collingwood 41n1
colonial x, 20, 25, 36–37, 40, 44n9,
    46–55 *passim*, 61n14–15, 62n17–18,
    63n24, 66, 99,
colonialism 6, 29–31 *passim*, 34, 44n9,
    54; *see also* settler-colonialism
coloniality x
community xi, 9, 21, 31, 58, 98
contestation 6, 34, 39, 48, 57; *see also*
    resistance
contingency xi, 6, 12, 17–18n10,
    40, 45
contradiction xi, 6–12 *passim*, 15n1,
    16n5, 17n7, 17n10, 19–25 *passim*,
    29, 30, 33, 36, 45, 53, 59n3, 68, 71,
    72, 87, 100, 101n12
contradictory *see* contradiction
cosmopolitanism x, xi, 40, 77, 82,
    91, 92
counter-colonial 27, 38; *see also*
    anti-colonial
counter-discourse 93–94
counter-Enlightenment 8, 9, 21

cultural *see* culture
culture 3, 7, 10, 13, 16n5, 20, 22–24,
    26–40 *passim*, 42n5, 42n8, 46–48,
    51, 52,54, 55, 60n10, 63n24, 70, 73,
    76, 87, 89, 92, 99

Dalit 2, 6, 12, 13, 16n5, 17n7,
    45–64, 99
decolonial x, 13, 20, 44n19
Delhi 71, 75, 77, 79, 80 *see also* New
    Delhi
democracy x, 17n9, 38, 43n11, 43n14,
    68, 93, 101–102n12
Derrida, Jacques 11
diachrony 23, 24, 26, 28
diaspora 31, 62n21, 70
difference *see* alterity; antinomies
Dirks, Nicholas 51, 61n14, 62n20
discipline 2, 3, 6–15, 18n13, 19–41,
    41–44nn1–20, 45, 51, 55, 59, 65, 66,
    72, 82, 87, 100
disenchantment 7, 10, 14, 17n7, 17n9,
    26, 86, 89, 90, 101n7
Dubois, Abbé 61n12
Dumont, Louis 49–51
Durkheim, Émile 25–27 *passim*,
    43n13, 91
dystopia 3, 4, 17n7, 17n9, 44n19,
    60n9, 73, 83, 94

elite 1, 4, 6, 7, 12, 13–14, 17n10, 65,
    66, 69–85, 97
elitism *see* scholasticism
embodiment 5, 16n6, 17n7, 47, 60n7,
    73, 88
Emergency (1975–77) 67–68, 70,
    83–84n5
emotion 9, 17n7, 18n14, 21, 23, 24,
    48, 90, 98
empire 3, 6–13 *passim*, 17n9, 17n10,
    19, 21, 24, 25, 31, 34, 36–37, 39, 40,
    41n1, 42n4, 52, 69, 90, 94, 97
enchantment x, 10, 17n9, 26, 55, 68,
    82, 86, 90, 98, 100, 101n7, 61n12,
episteme *see* epistemology
epistemic *see* epistemology
epistemology 2, 4, 11, 17n7, 23,
    41, 46
Enlightenment 6–13 *passim*, 17n9,
    19–22, 24, 37, 38, 40, 93, 97

entitlement 2, 16n5, 32, 86–91, 93,
98–100; *see also* elite
ethnography *see* anthropology;
discipline
ethnohistory 28
Euro-America x, 2, 25
Eurocentric x, 3, 96, 97
Europe ix, x, 4, 9, 21, 22, 25, 33, 36,
38, 41n1, 42n5, 59n3, 87, 93–97
passim, 102n14
European *see* Europe
Evans-Pritchard, E. E. 27, 28, 41n1,
41–42n2
everyday ix, x, 1–6 *passim*, 14, 43n14,
51, 53, 54, 61n11, 65, 66, 74, 84n9,
86–97 *passim*, 101n7
evolutionism 10, 22–24, 26
exceptionalisms 2–4, 14
exclusion 13, 16n5, 46, 51, 55–56,
61n12, 62–63n23, 63n24, 96,
102n12
exoticism 3, 31
extra-analytical 5, 90–99 *passim*,
101n7

Fabian, Johannes 6, 11, 21- 23, 26,
29, 73
Facebook 61n12, 66, 83n2
Febvre, Lucien 27
feminist 15n1, 29, 64n29, 94, 96,
101–102n12
fetish x, 11, 33
Foucault, Michel 11, 18n12, 18n14
France 21, 27, 32
friendship 1, 14, 47, 59n1, 71, 72,
75, 82
Fukuzawa, Hiroshi 62n17
functionalism 26–28

Gadamer, H-G 5
Gandhi, Indira 67–68
Gandhi, M. K. (Mahatma) 101 n7
Geertz, Clifford 29
gender 1, 11, 13, 17n7, 17n9, 17n10,
18n12, 20, 31, 34, 37, 38, 47, 48, 58,
63n28, 64n29, 65, 66, 72, 74, 77, 80,
82, 84n12, 89, 96, 102n12
genocide 6, 17n9
Germany 24, 33
Ghasidas, Guru 48

global south xi, 4
globalization x, xi, 3, 34
governmentality 45, 61n11, 61n15, 95
Guha, Sumit 60n10
Gumbrecht, Hans Ulrich x, 102n14
Gupta, Charu 46
Guru, Gopal 46, 60–61n10

Habermas, Jürgen ix, 93–97, 101–
102n12, 102n13
Haraway, Donna 15n1, 16n5
Harijan 61n11
von Herder, Johann Gottfried 22, 25
heritage 8, 13, 20, 36, 39–40, 41n1
hermeneutic ix, 16n5, 19, 22, 24, 25,
27, 83n3, 88
hierarchical *see* hierarchy
hierarchy 1, 3, 8, 10, 13, 16n5, 17n7,
18n12, 23, 25, 27, 41, 46–58 *passim*,
62n21, 66, 72–75, 81, 82, 84n9, 87,
89, 90, 93, 97–99
Hindu 50, 52, 54, 55, 63n28, 84n5
Hinduism 48, 56, 60n9, 61n11, 62n21,
63n28
historical anthropology 7, 12, 13, 34,
47, 65
historicism 22, 24–25, 26, 43nn10–11,
44n19
history ix, x, 4, 5, 7, 15n1, 16n4,
16n5, 17n7, 17n9, 18n14, 34–36,
46–48, 52–55, 56, 59n3, 60n9,
61n11, 61n12, 63n28, 70, 83, 87–88,
90, 93–100 *passim*, 102n14; *see also*
discipline
history without warranty 4, 88,
99–100
human sciences 2, 7, 10, 12, 18n12,
19, 20, 27, 28, 33, 41, 83n3

identity xi, 8, 16n5, 30, 31, 34, 38, 39,
45, 48, 52, 53, 57, 59n3, 63n28, 95
ideology 49–51, 60n9, 84n6, 87, 88,
90, 91
IIC *see* India International Centre
Ilaiah, Kancha 46, 61n12
immanence 2, 5–7, 12, 14, 15n1,
17n8, 48, 59, 60n7, 73, 86–100
passim, 101n7, 101n10
inclusion 13, 46, 55–56, 62–63n23
India International Centre 71, 79

indigeneity 8, 17n7, 17n10, 24, 31, 40, 42n9
International Relations 11
Islam 50, 60n9, 61n14, 63n28

Jaaware, Aniket 60n7

Kant, Immanuel 9, 22
Kapadia, Karin 58
Koopman, Colin, 18n14
Koselleck, Reinhart ix, 102n14

language 23, 36, 61n11, 93–95, 102n13
Latin America x, 2
law 11, 30, 34, 36, 47
life-worlds 1, 5, 14, 17n7, 87, 100
Lodhi Gardens 71, 77–80, 84n12

magic x, 30, 32, 68, 69, 70; *see also* antinomies
Mahima Dharma 61n11, 63 n26
Mahima Swami 48
Maine, Henry 23
Malinowski, Bronislaw 26
Mangoo Ram 48
market 10, 32, 66, 68–70 *passim*, 84n6, 90
Marx, Karl 25
Marxism 28, 30
Mazzarella, William 5
McCarthy, Thomas 94
Mencher, Joan 61n12
menstruation 58
mercantile 4, 6, 17n9, 43n14, 67, 68, 101n3
mercantilism *see* mercantile
Merleau-Ponty, Maurice 15, 100
Mevani, Jignesh 46
Mexico 79
Mexico City 91, 97
Michelet, Jules 43n11
microhistory 33
middle-class 17n10, 38, 68, 69, 72, 75–76, 79
Mintz, Sydney 28
Mohan, Sanal 46
modern *see* modernity
Modern School 14, 65, 69–70, 76, 84n7

modernity ix-xi, xiin1, 1–7, 16n3, 16n4, 17n9, 17–18 n10, 18n12, 18n14, 38–39, 43n12, 44n18, 45, 48, 50, 59n3, 61n15, 62–63n23, 69, 70, 74, 82, 83n3, 86–100 *passim*, 101n5; *see also* discipline
Moffatt, Michael, 49, 51, 61n12
Morgan, Lewis 23
myth 26, 47–48, 57, 64n29, 68, 98; *see also* antinomies
mythology 23, 68, 90
Muslim 68; *see also* Islam

Nagaraj, D. R. 59n1
Nandy, Ashis x
narrative 6, 11, 12, 17n9, 24, 26, 31–33, 35, 40, 43n11, 43n14, 54, 66–72 *passim*, 74, 88, 99, 100
nation x, xi, 3, 16n5, 17n10, 37–38, 44n20, 47, 55, 67, 69, 70, 76, 78, 80, 90, 95–99 *passim; see also* discipline
nationalism *see* nation
native 6–8, 13, 16n5, 20, 26, 41, 45, 51, 54, 55
nativism xi, 3
Nehru, J. L. 69
neoliberalism 13, 14, 16n5, 40, 65–71 *passim*, 72, 77, 80, 84n6, 84n7
New Delhi 14, 69–83 *passim*
Niebuhr, Barthold Georg 24
non-Brahman 49, 52, 57, 58
non-human 17n7, 35
non-Western 10, 17n10, 26–30, 34, 94, 97, 98
North Atlantic ix
Novetzke, Christian 63n26
Nuer people 27

ontological 17n7, 33, 37, 99
oppositions *see* antinomy
Ortner, Sherry 72–73
otherness 8, 23, 41
"ought" *see* scholasticism

pain 61n11
Pajnik, Mojca 94, 102n12
pandemic 15
Paraiyar 58
Parsuram 48

peasant 17n10, 29, 56, 67, 68
Periyar, E.V. R. N. 48
philosophy ix, 9, 12, 14, 24, 21, 25,
    39, 41n1, 87; *see also* Habermas,
    Jürgen
Phule, Jotirao 48
Pieper, Josef 101n3
political economy 14, 18n12, 28, 37,
    52, 60n10, 62nn17–18, 66–68
political science 10–11
politics xi, 13, 24, 26, 34–39 *passim*,
    43n11, 43n14, 44n18, 45–47, 59n3,
    60n9, 61n11, 62n21, 63n24, 66–68,
    70, 74, 76–79, 82–83, 84n6, 87–89,
    91, 94–95, 100; *see also* Dalit
pollution 49–58, 63n24
postcolonial 98; development 67–70,
    84n7; perspectives 13, 20, 33,
    44nn18–20; politics 49–50, 55,
    63n24
postfoundational 13, 18n14
postmodern 83n3, 98
poststructuralist 20
power x, 16n5, 74, 83, 101.n3, 17n7,
    17n10; *see also* alterity; antinomies;
    Dalit; discipline
practice 29–31, 36, 38, 46, 48–58
    passim, 60n7, 60n9, 62n20, 63n28,
    76, 87, 89, 90, 94, 100, 101n7
Prakash, Gyan 57
Prasad, Chandrabhan 47
primitive 6, 7, 25, 27
privilege *see* elite; entitlement
process 29–31
progress 11, 22, 24, 33, 35, 83,
    98–99
progressivism 7–10, 22–25, 27, 82
property 34, 67, 74, 80, 84–85 n13
public sphere 96, 101n2
purity *see* pollution; Sikhism

Quigley, Declan 51
quotidian xi, 15, 15n1, 55, 82, 99; *see
    also* everyday

race 6–10, 13, 15n1, 16n5, 17n7,
    18n12, 18n9, 19, 22–25, 31, 37–41
    passim, 62n21, 89
Radcliffe-Brown, A. R. 26
Raheja, G. G. 51

Rancière, Jacques 4, 43n11, 87,
    101n10
von Ranke, Leopold 24,
Rao, Anupama 46
rationalism/rationality *see* reason
Ravidas, Guru 48
Rawat, Ram N. 61n11
reason ix, 5–10, 13, 15n1, 16n6, 17n7,
    17n9, 16n14, 18n14, 20–24, 26,
    37, 40–41, 74, 83n3, 87, 88, 92–97,
    101n12; *see also* antinomies
Redfield, Robert, 28
Rege, Sharmila 46
religion 30, 34, 45; *see* also
    Christianity; Dalit
Renaissance 4, 42n4, 87
resistance 3, 4, 11, 73
Rhodes Livingstone Institute 28
ritual 11, 34; *see also* antinomies;
    Dalit
romantic *see* Romanticism
Romanticism ix, 7, 9, 10, 13, 19–24,
    101n7
romanticist *see* Romanticism

Said, Edward 44n18
Sant Nirmala 48
Sarukkai, Sundar 60–61n10
Satnamis 47, 54, 57, 61n11, 63n24
savage 13, 20, 23, 26, 41
Sawarkar, Savindra "Savi" 47, 59n2,
    63n23, 64n29
scholasticism 2–7, 12, 14, 15n1, 17n9,
    47, 49, 59, 71, 84n9, 86–100, 100n2,
    101n3, 101n4
secular 8, 40, 59n3, 101n4
secularization 17n9, 21
settler-colonialism 17nn9–10, 24, 25,
    36, 40, 41
sexuality 1, 13, 17n10, 20, 31, 37, 38,
    47, 48, 58, 71, 74, 80, 82, 89
Scheduled Caste 61n11
Scott, Joan 15n1
Sikhism 63n28
Simpson, Audra 16n5, 42–43n9
Skaria, Ajay 62n19
slavery 8, 17n9, 17n10, 20, 32, 40
social sciences 10, 29
socialism 69
sociology 10, 26, 32, 66

Sorayabai 48
sovereignty x, 40–41, 42n9
space 3, 8, 11, 13, 20, 26–27, 30,
    34–39, 53, 55, 59n3, 60n9, 74, 75,
    89, 90, 97, 100
spatial *see* space
Spencer, Herbert 23
spirit 35, 57, 99
state x, xi, 3, 8, 10, 13, 17n9, 20–21,
    34, 37–41 *passim*, 46–47, 52, 54–55,
    60n10, 66–69, 74, 77–79, 84n6,
    84–85n13, 91, 92, 98; *see also*
    antinomies
Stocking, George Jr. 22, 23, 42n5
structure 26, 27, 29–31, 43n12, 43n14,
    49–51, 61n12, 72, 75, 87, 90,
subaltern 3, 4, 13, 15n1, 17n10, 20, 28,
    34, 38–40, 54, 61n11, 82, 88, 97–99
subaltern studies 20, 32–34,
    44nn18–20
subject ix, xi, 1–7, 10, 12, 15,
    17–19n10, 18n12, 19–39 *passim*,
    43nn11–14, 47, 53, 54, 60n9, 66,
    69, 71–74, 82, 84n6, 84n11, 87–88,
    93–95, 101n5, 101n7
synchrony 26, 42n8

Taylor, Charles ix
telos 93–95
Teltumbde, Anand 46
theory 2, 4, 7, 8, 12, 14, 15n1, 17n9,
    29, 30, 61n10, 62n18, 66, 72, 86, 94,
    96–100, 101–102n12
Thorat, Sukhdeo 47
time 15, 21–27; *see also* anthropology;
    history; discipline; space

tradition 20, 24, 26, 28, 31, 34, 57,
    63n28, 66, 69, 82, 92, 96, 99; *see
    also* antinomies
transcendence 2, 3, 12, 14, 15n1,
    60n7, 87, 88, 92–95, 100n2,
    101n4
Trouillot, Michel-Rolph, 26
Tylor, Edward 23

United States of America *see*
    America
universal 3, 9, 17n7, 21, 23,
    24, 92
utopia 17n7, 83, 94

value properties *see* immanence
van Roermund, Bert 101n4
Vico, Giambattista 22
violence 6, 34
Viramma 58
Voltaire 22

Waghmore, Suryakant 46
Weber, Max 25
West ix-xi, 3–4, 9, 11, 17n10, 18n14,
    21, 22, 25–35 *passim*, 43n14, 61n10,
    69, 90, 92, 96–99
Western *see* West
White, Hayden 41n1
White, Stephen 94–95, 99
Wolf, Eric 28, 34
working-class 17n10
world system 30
Wright, Michelle M. 9, 22

Yengde, Suraj 46

For Product Safety Concerns and Information please contact our EU
representative GPSR@taylorandfrancis.com
Taylor & Francis Verlag GmbH, Kaufingerstraße 24, 80331 München, Germany

www.ingramcontent.com/pod-product-compliance
Lightning Source LLC
Chambersburg PA
CBHW061747270326
41928CB00011B/2402